James Alphonsus Dwyer

The Dominicans of Cork City and County

James Alphonsus Dwyer

The Dominicans of Cork City and County

ISBN/EAN: 9783741187872

Manufactured in Europe, USA, Canada, Australia, Japa

Cover: Foto ©Andreas Hilbeck / pixelio.de

Manufactured and distributed by brebook publishing software (www.brebook.com)

James Alphonsus Dwyer

The Dominicans of Cork City and County

The Dominicans of Cork City and County.

Church of St. Mary's, Pope's Quay, Cork.

The Dominicans of Cork City and County.

By REV. JAMES A. DWYER, O.P.

ILLUSTRATED.

Dominic was he called; and him I speak of
Even as of the husbandman whom Christ
Elected to his garden to assist him.
    DANTE *Paradiso*, XII. Canto, translated by Longfellow

CORK : PUBLISHED BY GUY AND COMPANY, LIMITED.
1896.

Dedication.

I DEDICATE this account of the Cork Dominicans to my revered Bishop, and beloved Brother in Christ, the MOST REV. THOMAS ALPHONSUS O'CALLAGHAN, O.P. Many years of close intimacy have enabled me to form a just appreciation of his noble qualities, therefore do I deem myself highly privileged in being permitted to place under his kind patronage this small tribute of love and esteem.

BR. JAMES ALPHONSUS DWYER, O.P.

St. Mary's Priory Cork,
    Feast of St. Dominic, 1896.

Preface.

INFLUENCED by the kindly expressed wishes of a few friends, I now publish in book form the account of my Cork Brethern. This volume includes not only what has lately appeared in the *Cork Historical and Archæological Journal*, but also some brief sketches of the Dominican houses of Youghal, Castlelyons, and Glanworth, which, like St. Mary's of the Isle, have either totally disappeared or stand in solitary ruins, still manifesting tokens of former glory and artistic beauty.

In connection with Youghal Convent is given a narrative of the miraculous statue of "Our Lady of Graces," now surmounting the Rosary Altar in the Church, Pope's Quay.

The appendix contains some documents which will doubtless prove a source of pleasure to the many friends and subscribers who have so kindly and generously helped me, and to whom I tender my sincere and heartfelt thanks.

Contents.

First Part—City.

INTRODUCTION

		PAGE
Chapter I. The Years of Prosperity		1
„ II. The Long and Dark Night of Persecution		6
„ III. The Dawn of a Brighter Day		21
„ IV. Unexpected Blessings		37
„ V. A Succession of Joys and Sorrows		52
„ VI. Great and Good Men		74

Second Part—County.

Youghal and the Miraculous Statue	113
Castlelyons—Convent of the Blessed Virgin	127
Glanworth—Convent of the Holy Cross	131
Conclusion	138

Appendix.

Three Important Occurrences	141
List of Deaths	143
Letter of Invitation received by Father Leahy to be present at the Synod of Thurles	145
Memorial of the Regulars of Ireland addressed to Members of both Houses of Parliament, April, 1829	146
Important Charge concerning the Catholic Religious Communities, delivered in the Rolls Court, Dublin, on the 3rd of November, 1864	150
The Religious Orders—The Penal Laws	167
The Penal Laws *versus* The Dominican Fathers	168
Our Lady of Youghal—"St. Mary of Graces"	186
INDEX	193

List of Illustrations.

		PAGE
1.	Church of St. Mary's, Pope's Quay, Cork	*frontispiece*
2.	South Elevation of St. Mary's Dominican Priory, Cork	24
3.	Interior of St. Mary's Church, Cork	25
4.	Dr. Hynes	39
5.	Father Jandel	43
6.	Rev. John Albert Ryan, S.T.M.	53
7.	Most Rev. Dr. Carbery, O.P.	77
8.	Rev. Thomas Burke, O.P.	81
9.	Most Rev. Dr. O'Callaghan, O.P.	85
10.	Most Rev. Dr. Hyland, O.P.	87
11.	Most Rev. Dr. Flood, O.P.	91
12.	Very Rev. B. T. Russell, O.P.	93
13.	Most Rev. Dr. Leahy, O.P.	95
14.	Convent of Youghal	115
15.	Friary of Youghal	117
16.	Statue and Old and New Shrine of Our Lady of Youghal	119
17.	Chalice of Youghal Convent	124
18.	Fac-simile Page of Black-Letter Bible	125
19.	Convent of Castlelyons	129
20.	Convent of Glanworth	133
21.	Doorway in Tower, Convent of Glanworth	135
22.	Sieur Boullaye le Gouz	187

Introduction.

"Let us now praise men of renown, and our fathers in their generation . . . men of great power, and endued with their wisdom. . . . Rich men in virtue, studying beautifulness; living in peace in their houses. All these have gained glory in their generations, and were praised in their days. . . . Their bodies are buried in peace, and their name liveth unto generation and generation. Let the people shew forth their wisdom, and the Church declare their praise."—*Ecclesiasticus*, chapter xliv.

DURING six hundred and sixty-seven years the Dominicans have resided in the city of Cork, and "through weal and woe" have the members of their Order ministered in unbroken succession to the spiritual wants of its people, nor did they hesitate to sacrifice themselves when necessary for the temporal welfare of those committed to their care.

For more than three centuries they remained unmolested in their home (St. Mary's of the Isle) on the banks of the Lee. But then persecution drove them from their peaceful cloisters, and obliged them to seek a place of safety where they could live in the observance of their rule, and at the same time labour for those endeared to them by many ties both of nature and religion. They, therefore, retired to "Old Friary Lane,"[1] situated off Shandon Street, where

[1] Gibson's *History of Cork*, page 371, vol. ii.

we find them in the early part of the eighteenth century, 1721, but they again moved off in 1784, and built a convent and chapel in Dominick Street, on the site now occupied by the Butter Crane. At length they settled down on Pope's Quay, where they carry on their priestly avocations for the benefit of the people of Cork and its neighbourhood.

Having thus given an outline of the chequered career of the Friars Preachers since their advent in our city, I propose to relate in detail what is known of their years of prosperity, then what befell them when scattered by the ruthless hand of persecution, and, finally, what comes under our observation in these days of comparative freedom, when the Dominicans are no longer hampered in the good work for which their founder established his Order—that of preaching and spreading the Gospel of Christ.

To effect this object I shall principally draw from the records of the Order in Cork,[2] and the *Hibernia Dominicana*.[3] When the information is from any other source, I shall indicate whence it comes.

[2] The *Abridged Annals of the Order of St. Dominic in Cork*, published in pamphlet form by the Very Rev. B. T. Russell, O.P., have furnished the materials of this historic account up to the opening of St. Mary's Church, Pope's Quay.

[3] Page 214.

The Dominicans of Cork City and County.

FIRST PART—CITY.

Chapter I.
The Years of Prosperity.

> Treading down this world of evil
>   To his mighty task he goes:
> Stript of all, he seeks the conflict,
>   Turns him to Christ's banded foes,
>   Grace sustaining,
>   With the fire that inward glows.
>
> Lo! his arms of heavenly temper—
>   Words and signs of wondrous power,
> Prayers of love, and tears of pity:
>   Whilst his warrior children bore
>   His commission
>   Onward still from shore to shore.—SAINT DOMINIC.

THE Order of Friars Preachers was introduced into Cork in 1229 by Philip Barry, a Welsh nobleman, and ancestor of the family of Barrymore, in the county of Cork. As a memorial of gratitude the members of the community placed in their church a bronze equestrian statue of the founder, which remained intact until the house was suppressed by

Henry VIII. This convent, dedicated to the Blessed Virgin, was erected on one of the marshes of the "five-isled city," and therefore called "Saint Mary's of the Island." The church is described in the history of the Order as a "magnificent church"—*Magnifica Ecclesia*. Of these buildings nothing now remains but some stones, which, at its erection, were inserted in the walls of the Priory, Pope's Quay.[4]

We know not the names or the number of the brethren when the community was first established, but their fame and credit had evidently spread, for early in their career David McKelly, a dignitary of the diocese of Cashel, joined the community, and we find that only eight years had elapsed since the foundation of St. Mary's when he was chosen bishop of Cloyne, and in the following year, 1238, was transferred to the metropolitan See of Cashel, of which he had previously been dean. He was replaced in the See of Saint Colman by another Dominican named Allan O'Sullivan. The new bishop showed his attachment for the Order by erecting, not far from his cathedral on the Rock of Cashel, a beautiful convent and church of Friars Preachers. He attended the first General Council

---

[4] These stones were given by the Corporation of Cork to the Very Rev. B. T. Russell, through the kind intervention of the late Mr. William Hegarty. A coign stone, likewise supposed to have belonged to St. Mary's of the Isle, and bearing this inscription—*In hoc signo vinces*—"In this sign shalt thou conquer," is to be found in one of the walls of the yard adjoining the mill of Mr. Edwin Hall, Crosse's Green; but the fact of this stone bearing a recent date causes a doubt as to its appertaining to the old Dominican foundation.

held in Lyons in 1245, and his name is to be seen subscribed to its acts. He died in 1252, after a distinguished career, equally remarkable for zeal and prudence. In the same year Allan O'Sullivan, bishop of Lismore, also departed this life.

The Dominican community of Cork was treated with special favour in 1309, an annual donation of thirty-five marks having been granted from the Royal Treasury. Some years afterwards (1317) the Friars, by the charter of Edward II. to the city of Cork, received the privilege of a free passage through the gate of the newly-erected city walls near their convent.[s] Similar grants were made to St. Mary's in the eighth year of the reign of Edward III. and subsequently. But when we reflect on the treatment given in after years by kings and nobles to the inmates of religious houses in Ireland, we are forcibly reminded of the wise counsel of the Psalmist, "Put not your trust in princes. . . . Blessed is he . . . whose hope is in the Lord his God."—*Ps.* 145.

As in the early history of the Order, its members were raised to the episcopate, so in the following century we find that Philip de Slane was bishop of Cork. About 1321 he was sent to Rome on a special embassy by the King of England, and subsequently appointed one of his Majesty's Council in Ireland. John le Bond who, in 1340, was prior of St. Mary's of the Island, had previously been dean of Cloyne,

---

[s] Gibson's *History of Cork*, page 368, vol. ii.

and was elected for the bishopric of Cork, but we cannot say that he accepted the dignity.[6]

Edmond Mortimer, Earl of March and Ulster, and father of the heir presumptive to the throne, coming to Cork when Lord Lieutenant of Ireland, took up his residence in the Dominican Convent. Whilst staying here he died on St. Stephen's Day, 1381, and is supposed to have been buried within the precincts of St. Mary's. A Cork Dominican, called therefore "Joannes Corcagiensis," was archbishop of Cologne in 1461. A certain citizen, named David Ferry, left by his will, drawn up about the year 1475, a legacy to the community of St. Mary's for masses for the dead. This legacy was mentioned amongst a number of bequests for repairing churches in Cork, damaged most likely during the disturbances which had occurred in the city.

In course of time various circumstances combined in causing the rule to be somewhat relaxed amongst the brethren in Ireland. The principal cause of this was the War of the Roses. Thence arose in our city civil disturbances unfavourable to strict discipline. To remedy this relaxation it was ordained in the General Chapter of Milan, in 1484, that the Very Rev. Maurice Moral, then Vicar-General of the Dominican Order in Ireland, should re-establish strict observance in the Cork convent, as likewise in the other houses under his jurisdiction. The brethren most willingly

---

(6) *Monasticon Hibernicum:* Archdall, page 57.

submitted to the directions of their superior, and we are assured that fourteen years afterwards, in 1508, the Reform—as exact conventual life is called—was in a most flourishing condition in St. Mary's of the Island. In the following year the Dominican communities of Cork, Youghal, Limerick, and Coleraine were formed into a "congregation of strict observance," under the authority of a vicar-general. This arrangement was highly approved of by those assembled in the General Chapter of Rome, A.D. 1518.

An event of great importance took place in 1536. Pope Paul III. made Ireland, hitherto under the jurisdiction of the Provincial of England, a separate Province of the Order. The Irish brethren then elected their own local Superior, or Provincial. This privilege was accepted and acknowledged by the General, and was the means of providentially saving the Dominicans of Ireland from utter extinction—a fate which befell the English branch of the Order at the dissolution of religious houses in the reign of Henry VIII.

Chapter II.
The Long and Dark Night of Persecution.

When heresy swept o'er the land like a destroying flood,
And tyrants dipped their reeking hands in the martyr's sacred blood—
The sons of Dominic then like men embraced the stake and stood
Before the burning pile as 'twere the Saviour's holy rood,
And kissed their scapulars whilst they bled, three hundred years ago.

And when the altar fed the flame and Christ was mocked again,
Then faithful voices still were heard o'er mountain, cave, and glen,
And thus was saved our country's faith, and thus the Lamb was slain;
And ne'er was Ireland's title more "the Isle of Saints" than when
The Preacher found a martyr's grave, two hundred years ago.
—Rev. T. Burke, o.p.

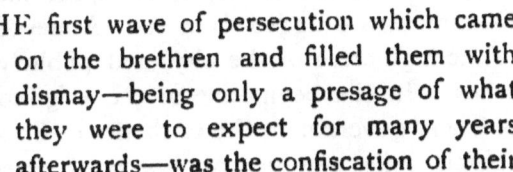

THE first wave of persecution which came on the brethren and filled them with dismay—being only a presage of what they were to expect for many years afterwards—was the confiscation of their convent, with all its appurtenances, and its sale to a person named William Boureman at an annual head rent of six shillings and ninepence. This act of injustice was perpetrated under Henry VIII. For a long time afterwards the Dominicans resided in their house, and, though frequently compelled to take to flight or conceal themselves, they never despaired of regaining possession of their cherished abode ; and, strange to say, they contrived at intervals to live in community in St. Mary's of the Isle during the troublesome times which intervened between this act of confiscation and the accession of William III. In the meantime Peter Wall, of the Order of Saint Dominic, was nominated bishop of Cloyne by Pius IV. in 1556.

An act of vandalism was committed during the reign of Elizabeth, in 1578, to the great grief of the Catholics who witnessed it. By order of Mathew Sheyne, Protestant bishop of Cork, the image of Saint Dominic was dragged from the "Abbey of the Isle" to the high cross of the city, and publicly burned to ashes. In the beginning of the reign of James I., to whose government the Catholics of Cork refused to submit whilst deprived of "liberty of conscience," the friars began to repair their church and convent ; but persecution soon obliged them, as well as others, to abandon the repairing of the old churches and abbeys. In 1606 the Lord President of Munster subjected the Mayor, Aldermen, and other persons of the city of Cork to heavy fines, and even imprisonment, for refusing to assist at Protestant service. In the thirteenth year of James I. (1616) a grant was made to Sir John King of the church, steeple, monastery, etc., of the Cork Dominicans. In the following year stringent proclamations were passed, condemning the regular clergy to banishment and outlawry.[7] We find it asserted in the Acts of the General Chapter of Rome in 1644, that, four years previously, a Middle Chapter of the Dominicans of Ireland was held in the Cork convent, and that Father James O'Hurley, subsequently bishop of Emly, presided. Several of the other Fathers present soon became illustrious as bishops, or martyrs for the Faith. About the same time a distinguished preacher named Father John O'Morrogh was attached to this house.

In 1641 the Irish Catholics arose in self-defence, and the following year the Dominican Order, renewing its youth like the phœnix of romance, was completely restored throughout Ireland. In the short interval of peace enjoyed by the Catholics, there were forty-three houses in a flourishing condition and six hundred Friars Preachers in the country; but how soon, alas! were these either dispersed or murdered. Three years afterwards Lord Inchiquin gave orders that the Catholics of Cork be expelled from the city;[8] and ere long, the rage of blind fanatics burst forth in all its fatal virulence, especially against the members of the religious bodies, many of whom received the martyr's crown, for they were mindful of that inspired

[7] About the year 1630 there were many persons who, in order to be exempt from the "sessa" of soldiers and other public charges, took up their residence on the island of St. Mary's. Hence it would seem that the island was free from taxation, and that its freedom was acknowledged by the authorities.

[8] Gibson's *History of Cork*, p. 77, vol. ii.

admonition: "Strive for justice for thy soul, and even unto death fight for justice."—*Ecles.* iv. 33.

In order to understand what the brethren endured in those dark and trying times, and what glorious fortitude they evinced in their sufferings, it will be sufficient to describe the noble conduct of but a few of those champions of truth and liberty.

Father Richard Barry, a Cork Dominican, having in 1647 courageously defended the sanctuary in the Cathedral of Cashel, where he was Prior, and refused to divest himself of his religious dress for that of a secular (as he considered doing so an act of apostacy), was ordered to be burned alive on the Rock of Cashel. Having suffered for two hours with wonderful heroism, he was pierced through with a sword. Four days after this shocking occurrence, when the English soldiers had left the town, the proofs of his martyrdom were judicially examined by the Vicar-General and the Notary Apostolic. His remains were then conveyed in solemn procession, and with joyful anthems, to the beautiful enclosure of his own convent, where it is hoped they still remain in undisturbed repose.

Only one year elapsed after this distinguished martyr had gone to his reward, when a young Dominican, Brother Dominic de Burgo, a near relative of the Earl of Clanricarde, was captured on board the ship in which he intended to sail for Spain in order to pursue his studies, and was cast into prison at Kinsale, whence he escaped by jumping from the wall to the sea-shore. Covered with mire, without food, drink, or sufficient clothing, he concealed himself for two days in a neighbouring wood, and was then sheltered under the hospitable roof of the family of the Roches, probably of Garretstown. In after life he became the celebrated Bishop of Elphin, for whose head or capture the Government offered a reward. Oliver Plunket, the martyred Archbishop of Armagh, wrote from his dungeon warning him of the attempts made against his life by the Privy Council. He died an exile from his beloved country. Another martyr to his Master's cause was Father Æneas Ambrose O'Cahill, an eloquent preacher, and a man of great zeal. Recognised by a troop of Cromwell's soldiers as a member of the Dominican community of Cork, they cut him to pieces with their sabres, scattered his limbs, and trampled them under foot. This occurred in 1651.

The General Chapter, held in Rome five years subsequently, described in one of its Acts the furious persecution which had been raging for a considerable time in Ireland, and gives us to understand its fatal results in the following expressive words:—" An abundant harvest of those, who in our Irish province have suffered for the Catholic faith, has been gathered in these our days into the celestial granary; since of forty-three convents which the Order possessed in this island, not a single one survives to-day, which the fury of the heretical persecutor hath not either burned or levelled to the ground, or diverted to profane uses.

In these religious establishments there were counted about six hundred, of whom but the fourth part is now in the land of the living, and even that number is dispersed in exile; the remainder died martyrs at home, or were cruelly transported to the island of Barbadoes."

In the meantime there was one who on account of the disturbed state of the country appears to have escaped the notice of even his superiors. Father Thomas Fitzgerald, full of zeal and piety, as well as great simplicity of manners, assumed the garb of a peasant, and thus attired exercised his sacred ministry amongst the Catholics of Cork during the entire period of Cromwell's usurpation. Another Cork Dominican, Father Eustace Maguire, was distinguished not only for similar qualifications of piety and zeal, but also for fearless courage. He was chosen governor of the castle of Druineagh, near Kanturk, and defended it so bravely during the Cromwellian wars that it was never captured, nor did it surrender. When Charles II. was restored, the Regulars set about building new convents, or repairing those left standing in retired places. Novices were even received and professed.

About this period the Church of St. Mary's of the Isle—then changed into a barn—the spire and convent, etc., were handed over to Captain Arthur Dillon as a grant in trust for the "forty-nine" officers who had served in King Charles's army. Notwithstanding this, the Dominicans soon regained possession of their property.

A beautiful silver remonstrance, bearing date 1669, and the name of the donor, Father Richard Kent, O.P., is still used at Benediction of the Blessed Sacrament in the Dominican Church, Pope's Quay. A silver crucifix, [9] on which is inscribed the same date, was presented to St. Mary's of the Isle by Father John O'Regan, O.P., who is described in the History of the Order in Ireland as " a distinguished preacher of the Word of God." The most precious treasure, however, in the hands of the Cork Dominicans is the miraculous statue of Our Lady of Youghal, " St. Mary of Graces," which is publicly venerated in their church, and of which an account is given in the second part of this book.

In a Chapter held at Athenry, county Galway, in 1676, Father Constantine O'Keeffe, of the Cork community, was chosen Provincial of Ireland. He was a profound theologian, an eloquent preacher and poet in the Irish language. He endured great trials and sufferings in the time of Cromwell, and died in 1679.

In the previous year the Regulars, as well as other ecclesiastics, were ordered by the authorities to leave the kingdom within a month. This order was given on the 18th October, and on the 20th of the following month, the day appointed for their expatriation, public notice was issued forbidding any Catholic whatsoever to reside in the city of Cork. To add to this outrageous treatment, the magistrates were in the

---

(9) Also in possession of the present community.

succeeding year commanded to close all places of Catholic worship.(10)

When James II. landed at Kinsale, and thence came to Cork, he lodged at St. Mary's of the Isle, and on the following Sunday assisted at mass in the Franciscan church of the North Abbey, situated on what is now known as the North Mall.

On the accession of William, Prince of Orange, the Friars Preachers were compelled to leave their convent, because of the unjust laws enacted by him against the Catholic clergy and people, and never after did they resume possession of it. Their island home then became the residence of the Mayor of Cork, and in after years, though called "the great house of St. Dominic," was used by the Earl of Inchiquin as his town mansion.

Amongst the inmates of St. Mary's of the Isle at the time of their flight and dispersion was Father William Barry, who, having studied at Toulouse and taught philosophy, returned to Cork, where he became eminent as a preacher both in Irish and English. He was several times elected prior by the brethren. After the dethronement of James II., having suffered much in the persecutions since 1680, he fled to Louvain, where he was chosen prior of the Holy Cross Convent, which belonged to the Irish province. This convent he enlarged and beautified, and at the expiration of his term of office was elected prior of the English

---

(10) A registry of the Dominicans of Ireland from 1683 to 1696 is preserved in the Cork house.

Dominicans of Bornheim, in the Low Countries. He died in 1706. Father Peter O'Garavain, who had been professor of philosophy in Portugal, was the last superior of St. Mary's of the Isle. On his return to Ireland he was appointed head of the Cork community, and when the city was captured by King William's army he fled to Lisbon, where he was chosen rector and professor of theology in the Irish College of Corpo Santo. He died exiled from his native country. [11]

An Act of Parliament was passed in 1697, ordering all dignitaries and regular clergy to leave the country, and forbidding them to return under pain of death. As a consequence many prelates and friars were transported, or went into voluntary exile. No monastic house in Ireland was left untouched—not one but was suppressed. Still, rather than desert the persecuted Catholics, many of the friars fled to the mountains, concealed themselves in caverns, or were protected by kind-hearted Protestants.

It is related that at this time a Cork Dominican, Father John Morrogh, unable through illness to escape, was taken prisoner and lodged in the city jail, where he found rest in death after four years of hardship and confinement. About the same period Father Walter Fleming arrived in Cork, whence he sailed to France, accompanied by Father O'Heyn, author of the Dominican history, *Epilogus Chronologicus*. In

---

[11] In 1706.

the following year the former returned to Ireland with Father Daniel McDonnell, a brother Dominican, but before landing both were seized and cast into Cork jail, where they were kept in chains for more than a year. On regaining liberty they returned to France. Another worthy of notice was Father James Barrett, who had been married, and becoming a member of the Order after his wife's death was ordained priest in Cork. He was highly connected in this county, and at the time of the banishment of the clergy was advanced in years. Assuming the dress of a herdsman, he took refuge in the house of an English friend, at the same time exercising his sacred ministry in the neighbourhood with great fruit. He died a peaceful death in the year 1710.[12]

A visitation was made in 1704 by Father Ambrose O'Connor, who had been appointed Provincial of the Irish Dominicans, whilst in Spain. Though sought after by spies, he escaped unhurt, and without being interfered with in his mission through the country. In the report of his visitation drawn up for Pope Clement IX., he informed his Holiness that there were ninety Dominican missionaries who, though concealed, were actively engaged in the ministry, and that five were in prison suffering for the faith.

About the time of the Hanoverian succession, the

[12] About the beginning of the eighteenth century an exception was made by the Government in favour of secular priests, on condition that they register their names at quarter sessions. Should they fail to do so, they were to receive treatment similar to that of the regular clergy, for whom there was no mercy.

persecution somewhat abated, and the Dominicans scattered throughout Ireland began cautiously to form themselves into communities. Therefore, in 1721, we find the brethren of Cork, with Father Peter McCarthy as Prior, living in a narrow lane off Shandon Street, which on that account is still called Old Friary Lane.[13]

The registry of professions for this convent dates from 1722. Another book, bearing date 1730, also exists, in which are ascribed the names of those received into the Third Order of St. Dominic, the Confraternities of the Rosary of the Blessed Virgin and the Sacred Name of Jesus. In this book are likewise to be found the names of deceased benefactors. Father Thomas Loghlin, preacher and confessor to the late dethroned king, was prior in 1730.

In the succeeding year a Committee was appointed by the House of Lords to enquire into the state of Catholicity in Ireland ; and of the religious houses that had existed in the city of Cork only one Friary was returned in the report, the number of the community being unknown. This was evidently the house in Friary Lane. The following resolution was passed by the Committee :—" That it is our opinion that the number of popish priests, monks, and friars, and of public Mass-houses and convents, has of late years greatly increased in this kingdom, to the manifest danger of the Protestant religion of his Majesty's

---

[13] The name had for some years been effaced, but has recently been restored by the Corporation, through the kind intervention of Mr. Michael McCarthy and the late Mr. John O'Brien, T.C.

Government, and of the peace and welfare of this kingdom."

It is pleasing to notice that, notwithstanding these apprehensions, several novices received the Dominican habit, and were afterwards admitted to solemn profession in the Cork convent. Amongst others were the Brothers Albert O'Brien, Nicholas Walsh, Thomas Hylan, John Fitzgerald, Dominic Morrogh, John Lynch, Dominic McCurtin, and Dominic Walsh, all of whom were professed between the years 1722 and 1735.[14] We are informed that in 1751 the Provincial applied to the General of the Order for authority to establish a novitiate in Cork. Eleven years afterwards postulants were sent abroad to receive the habit and to study for this house. Daniel Albert O'Brien, first-mentioned amongst those affiliated to the old Friary, went to Louvain, where, having finished his scholastic course, he was appointed professor of philosophy and regent of studies. Returning subsequently to Ireland he laboured zealously in Cork and Limerick, being remarkable as a preacher both in English and Irish.

The See of Cork was separated from that of Cloyne in 1748, and Dr. Richard Walsh, bishop of Cork, entrusted to Father O'Brien the pastoral charge of the South Parish,[15] and also appointed him vicar-general. Finding that the chapel, a thatched building on the

[14] *Hibernia Dominica*, p. 216.

[15] In those days Dominicans held several parishes in Ireland, there not being a sufficient number of secular priests.

site now occupied by the Presentation monastery and schools, was unfit for Divine worship, the good pastor, nothing daunted by the bigotry of the times, nor dismayed by the difficulties in his path, undertook to erect the present parish church, which he completed in 1766. When all things were in order he resigned the parish in 1774, and was succeeded by Dr. Francis Moylan, subsequently bishop of Cork. Father O'Brien returned to his convent in Friary Lane, where, after seven years of prayer and labour, he passed to his eternal reward.

The members of the Friary Lane community were remarkable for their varied learning. Amongst them were Father John O'Mahony, who was regent of studies and professor of Scripture at Louvain; Father John Lynch, who filled the chair of philosophy in Rome, and was likewise master in Saint Thomas's College, Seville; Father Dominic Morrogh, who taught philosophy for two years, was then master of studies and second regent; and Father William Lonergan, who besides being rector of the College of Corpo Santo, taught the entire ecclesiastical course both in Lisbon and Louvain. But the brethren of this house were not less remarkable for their assiduity in the confessional as well as their zeal in the pulpit, and as a consequence their chapel was much frequented by devout persons, one of whom—Miss Nano Nagle, foundress of the Presentation Order—deserves special notice, her name being held in benediction by the Irish people. She and her brother, Councillor Joseph Nagle, presented to the Old Friary a handsome tabernacle, surmounted by a canopy, for exposition of the Blessed Sacrament. This valued gift is still preserved by the Cork community.

As no direct opposition was feared on the part of the authorities, a new convent and chapel were built by the Friars Preachers in 1784. The site chosen was that on which the historic Shandon castle formerly stood, and where, as already mentioned, the butter crane was subsequently erected. There are many still living in the city who cherish a fond and grateful remembrance of Dominick Street Friary and its inmates during fifty-five years devoted to the interests, both spiritual and temporal, of those who frequented their beautiful chapel. Two members of this community were chosen by Bishop Moylan to teach theology in the Ecclesiastical Seminary, established in Cork during his episcopate—Father Conway, who had been lecturer of philosophy in the College of Corpo Santo, Lisbon, and Father John Sheehan, who was prior of the Irish Dominican Convent of Holy Cross, Louvain, at the invasion of the French army during the Revolution. Dr. Nugent, provincial, was at this time appointed parish priest of Mitchelstown, and vicar-general of the diocese of Cloyne.

Though the Emancipation Act of 1829 was passed for the relief of the Catholic people of Ireland, its benefits did not extend to the regular clergy, who soon after experienced the same persecuting spirit manifested by the clauses of the Charitable Bequests Bill, which has since been occasionally enforced against them when their rights were in question. They were, nevertheless, content to minister to the spiritual wants of the people, and to fulfil the sacred obligations which, as religious, they had voluntary contracted. The secular clergy and faithful people of Cork held public meetings to protest against this petty intolerance of the Government, but their protestations were unheeded, and to this day ban and proscription remain on the statute book, and have been frequently brought forward in courts of justice, even in recent years, to the detriment of the regulars.[16]

[16] The regulars were excepted in "Relief Bill" passed on 13th of April, 1829, by a clause for the gradual suppression of the Jesuits and monastic orders. Religious establishments of females were allowed to exist.

Public General Statutes, 1829. 10º Georgii IV., cap. 7. "An Act of Relief of His Majesty's Roman Catholic Subjects."

Chapter III.
The Dawn of a Brighter Day.

> Saith Saint Dominic to his chosen,
> "If the seed be put to keep,
> It will moulder to corruption,
> And no fruit shall any reap."
>
> Saith Saint Dominic to his chosen,
> "If the seed be cast abroad,
> It will bring forth in due season
> For the reaping of the Lord."—ELLEN DOWNING,
> otherwise "Mary of the Nation."

THE foundation stone of St. Mary's Church, Pope's Quay, was laid without public ceremony at the close of a memorable day of the year 1832; but this silent act of religion signified that the time was not far distant when the Dominicans of Cork would once more rejoice in the possession of peace and prosperity. Seven years had passed, and fleeting clouds were still visible on the horizon, but it may be said that the dense darkness of ceaseless persecution to which all "Regulars" were subjected had come to an end. On the auspicious occasion of the solemn dedication of St. Mary's church, in the year 1839, many Irish bishops, as likewise the Provincials of three

religious orders, attended the celebration. The Most Rev. Dr. Crolly, archbishop of Armagh and Primate of all Ireland, preached, the ceremony being performed by the Right Rev. Dr. Murphy, bishop of Cork, assisted by the Most Rev. Dr. Egan, of Kerry ; Dr. Foran, of Waterford ; Dr. French, O.P., of Kilmacduagh and Kilfenora ; Dr. Kinsella, of Ossory ; Dr. Healy, of Kildare and Leighlin ; Dr. Hynes, O.P., of Zante and Cephalonia ; and Dr. Crotty, of Cloyne and Ross. A sumptuous banquet was given by the citizens to the bishops and other distinguished persons, amongst whom was the " Liberator," Daniel O'Connell, who presided. A full account of the proceedings was published in the London, Dublin, and provincial Press.[17]

For nine years the brethren officiated in their new church, whilst residing in Dominick Street, when in 1848 the foundation stone of the present Priory was laid by the late Most Rev. Dr. Delany, in presence of a large concourse of priests and laity. A description

[17] To perpetuate the memory of the dedication of St. Mary's, Pope Gregory XVI. decreed, by rescript from the Sacred Congregation of Indulgences, Rome, dated 19th November, 1841, that the anniversary be celebrated with an octave, commencing on the Sunday immediately following the Feast of St. Luke, which falls on the 18th October. A plenary indulgence was granted to the faithful who, having received the Sacraments, would visit the church on the anniversary, or any day during the octave, and pray for the intentions of his Holiness. The same indulgence was likewise granted on the above conditions to all persons who assisted at the annual solemn commemoration of the deceased benefactors of the Church of St. Mary's, the celebration to take place on any day within the Octave of "All Souls," appointed once and for ever by the Bishop of Cork. It was therefore fixed on the Monday after "All Souls' Day."

of the ceremony was given in the *Cork Examiner* of the 3rd May, as follows :—

"The foundations were traced out in lines of masonry of great extent. After the Litany of the Saints was chanted, his Lordship sprinkled the first stone and foundation with holy water. A silver trowel, used at the foundation of the Metropolitan Church in Dublin, was then presented to his Lordship by the architect, William Atkins, esq., on a massive silver salver; when his Lordship, taking the trowel, signed the mark of the cross on the corners of the stone and laid the mortar. The stone was then let down into its berth, the foundations were again sprinkled with holy water, and the ceremony was concluded. In a hollow of the stone had been placed a bottle containing a parchment scroll and two beautiful medallions—one of the coronation of Queen Victoria ; the other, an exquisite specimen of art, of the installation of the reigning Pontiff, presented by Dr. Delany for the occasion. These two medals, as it were, typified the spiritual allegiance paid by the founders to the head of the Catholic Church and the allegiance due and paid to the temporal Sovereign. The parchment bore the following inscription :—

"Jesus—Maria—Dominicus. Hujus cœnobii fratrum Prædicatorum sub titulo Sanctœ Mariæ fundamentum jecit, benedixitque Illustrissimus et Reverendissimus Gulielums Delany, D.D., Episcopus Corcagiensis, assistente clero utriusque Ordinis, populoque hujusce civitatis plaudente, in festo S. Athanasii Doctoris Ecclesiæ, Pio Nono Pontifice Maximo Ecclesiam gubernante, Victoria Regina Nostra feliciter regnante, Provincialé Hib. Dom., Adm. R. P. Patritio Dunn, etc., etc., etc.'

[TRANSLATION].

"Jesus—Mary—Dominic. The foundation stone of this Convent of Friars-Preachers, under the invocation of St. Mary, was laid and blessed on the Feast of St. Athanasius, Doctor of the Church, in the year of our Lord 1848, by the Most Illustrious and Most Reverend Bishop of Cork, William Delany, D.D., in the

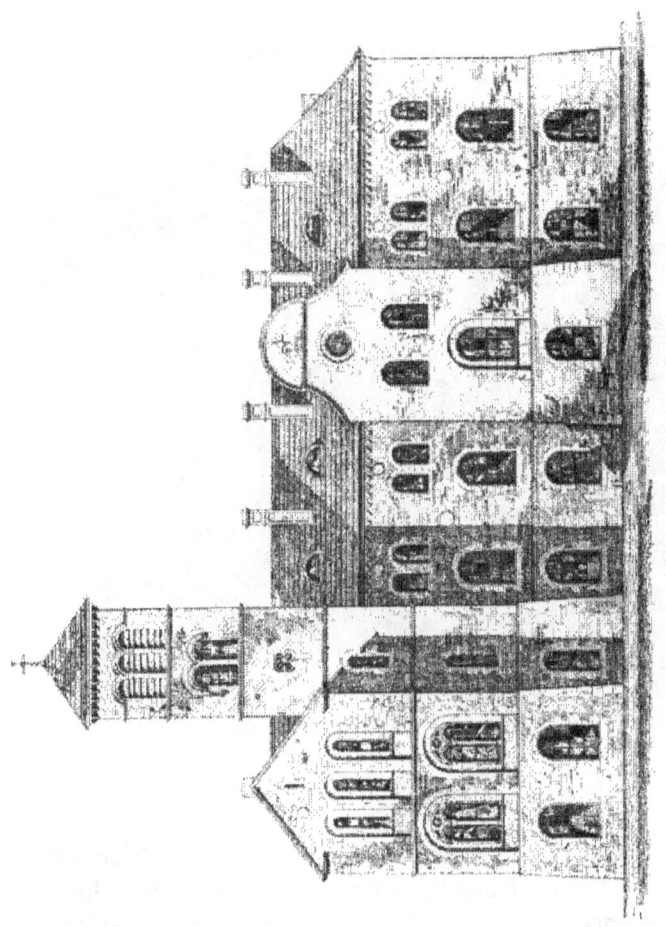

South Elevation of St. Mary's Dominican Priory, Cork.

Pontificate of Pius IX., in the reign of Queen Victoria, during the Provincialship of the Very Rev. Father Brother Patrick Dunn.

"It also bore the names of the Prior and Fathers of the Community, with the architect and principal contractors."

INTERIOR OF ST. MARY'S CHURCH, CORK.

When the ceremony was concluded, the Prior, Very Rev. B. T. Russell, delivered an eloquent address, the appearance of which in extenso will, doubtless, be hailed by our readers with unmingled feelings of satisfaction.

Address.

"In returning thanks for your lordship's presence and blessing on this occasion, I express the gratitude not only of a community devotedly attached to the rule and person of their Bishop, and, may I be permitted to add, their much-loved and honoured friend, but also of every superior and member of the Dominican Order in Ireland. Long and anxiously, my lord, have we been expecting the interesting ceremony of this day; and now, in the name of the entire Irish province of Friars Preachers, I hail the episcopal benediction that has just descended on the foundations of St. Mary's Priory as initiatory to the restoration of the discipline and usefulness of our ancient Institute in this country. To you, Very Rev. and Rev. Brethren, who have favoured us with your attendance, we can offer no acknowledgment more acceptable than to assure you of the reciprocity of our cordial and respectful attachment, 'careful,' as you know we have ever been, ‹to keep with you the unity of the spirit in the bond of peace.' We have no other return, fellow-citizens, to make to you for your friendly sympathies with us on this, as on every other occasion, than, under the sense of this new obligation, to labour more strenuously than ever for the spiritual welfare of yourselves and your families.

"The erection of the structure, of which the ground lines are now traced before us, has been undertaken with no other motive than to prepare a meet dwelling-place for the introduction into our conventual life of a new and improved system of regular observance; or, to speak with more truth and propriety, for the return and re-instatement of the primitive spirit of the Order of St. Dominic, such as it had flourished in Cork more than six hundred years ago, when, for the reception of the first Dominican community, the walls of old 'St. Mary's Abbey of the Island' arose on the southern banks of the Lee, under the protecting shadows of the mystic round tower and venerable Cathedral of St. Finbarr, the founder and patron saint of this city. To us who have long entertained those desires of renewed monastic life—

impaired, as it could not but have been amongst us by the effects of penal restrictions and the unfavourable circumstances of the country; to us, who in 1832 laid the foundations of St. Mary's Church, with a view to the eventual establishment on this adjoining spot of our Order in its original integrity—how auspicious is the coincidence that we have found ourselves ready to commence the work of renovation at a moment when Pius IX. has issued an encyclical letter to the Superiors of all Religious Orders throughout the Catholic world, a copy of which was addressed to our Irish Dominican Provincial, expressive of the warmest paternal affection for the regular clergy, and breathing from the heart of our Holy Father an anxious wish—to use the words of his' Holiness—'that in every religious community may be so revived, as to flourish and to prosper from day to day, integrity of morals, holiness of life, the observance of regular discipline, the cultivation of letters and holy knowledge, and above all the laws peculiar to each Order; that thus may be maintained in each religious family a fervent and vigorous vitality, usefulness to the people secured, the Divine worship upheld, and the glory of God more and more augmented.' Thus, you see, my friends, that in the breast of the great and good Pontiff the Apostle's 'daily instance and solicitude for all the churches' is not suppressed under the weight 'of those things which are without'—accumulated and increasing political anxieties. The same voice which has recently issued forth from the depths of the sanctuary, to herald the new mission of the Church in its gospel of truth and order and blessedness to society, hallowing with the benedictions of heaven every nationality which is founded or reconstructed by the spontaneous power of the popular will—that imposing voice is now heard in our monastic solitudes, bidding us, who are exempted by our state of life from the politics as from the pleasures of the world, to build up again our desolate places, and to make the ways of the desert bloom again as the flowering Carmel. Never was an admonition from the Chair of Peter more opportune and salutary. We are fallen on times of mighty portent and marvellous changes, of which the issues are not known. For religious truth, new conflicts may have soon to be encountered ; for religious devotedness, new sacrifices demanded ; for religious triumphs, new heroism called forth. At no former period of church history was it more needful that all the forces of religion should be closely united, compactly arrayed, skilfully marshalled. Every element of spiritual power, however minute or isolated, may, by its attraction to the great centre of unity in counsel and action, be made subordinate to some general good ; and thus, too, may be rendered useful to society and the Church, in their new relations, even the services of one small religious community, and still more the combined energies of a scattered religious order. Is it then to be wondered at that, while national and municipal guards are encompassing the seats of reorganised political empire with strength and safety, the greatest reformer of the age should summon to the aid and glory of Christ's spiritual kingdom on earth those religious orders which, as Pius IX. himself writes, ' compose in their several forms that magnificent variety which invests the Church with such great lustre, and constitute those auxiliary troops, those chosen battalions of Christ, who have always been amongst the most distinguished ornaments and the firmest bulwarks of religion and of the State.'

" To inspire amongst us, the regular clergy of modern times, an emulous imitation of the virtues, learning, utility, and devotedness of our religious predecessors, the Holy Pontiff recalls to our memories the services which our spiritual fathers in their generations rendered to religion in all its high paths of literature, in its perpetual contributions to civilization, in its ministrations to suffering humanity under every shape, in its uncompromising conflicts with error, in its propagation of the faith, and the enlightenment and sanctification of the people ; and when his Holiness recalls specially to our remembrance how those who went before us ' combatted bravely and suffered joyfully all kinds of cruelties, torments, punishments and deaths,' I cannot but think of the days of the tyrannical and sacrilegious dissolution of our own once flourishing conventual establishments in Ireland—sanctuaries of piety, nurseries of learning, storehouses of charity for the poor—all plundered and prostrated in ruin. I think of the expelled and persecuted friars; and not to stray from the annals and traditions of our own Convent of St. Mary's in Cork, I think of many of the old Fathers of this house, who like the Prophets of old 'were put to death by the sword, they wandered about in sheep-skins and goat-skins, being in want, distressed, and afflicted, of whom this world was not worthy, wandering in deserts, in mountains and in dens and the caves of the earth.'

"I think, for instance, of the great Irish martyr in the days of the Regicides, Father Richard Barry, of this city and Convent, who rather than stain the white habit of St. Dominic, which he had worn without a blemish from his youth, when offered life in exchange for one word of apostacy to his Church, or one deed of disloyalty to his country, suffered himself to be bound to a stake on the top of the Rock of Cashel and to be burned alive, and to writhe in the tortures of the fiery ordeal for two hours, until a sword pierced his side, and the gushing heart's-blood quenched the flames in which his soul was purified for heaven. I think of the eloquent preacher of Cork, in his days, Father Eneas Ambrose O'Cahill, who, when known to be a Friar of our Dominican Convent, was rushed on, though armless and unoffending, by a troop of ferocious and fanatical cavalry, and crushed under the hoofs of horses, and mangled to pieces with ruthless sabres, and butchered in the streets until his corpse rolled on the pavement a gory and mutilated trunk. I think of the pious and chivalrous Father Eustace Maguire, called by the historian a second Machabeas, who for eleven years defended against the assaults of the enemies of his country and creed the ancient castle of Dromagh, still standing near Kanturk. I think of the venerable Prior of our house, Father John Morrogh, who, when unable to escape the hot pursuit of the persecutor by a timely flight with many of his brethren across the seas, was seized and dragged into a felon's cell in the gaol of Cork, and there, after four years of merciless treatment, was delivered by death for the enjoyment of the confessor's crown in a better world. I think, in fine, of Father James Barrett, a man of noble birth in this country, who, to the honour of generous Protestants be it not untold or forgotten, was sheltered from the priest-hunters under the hospitable roof of an old Protestant friend, where he lay long concealed, unbetrayed and unnoticed, in the coarse frieze dress of a herdsman, seldom venturing abroad unless when under the covert of the night-darkness the good old gentleman, the pious priest of a suffering God, would go forth to visit the dying poor with the rites and consolation of their holy religion. Oh! how can we forget such memories at a moment like this when the shadows of the historical past are mingling along the line of these foundations with the sunshine of the present and the still brighter prospects of the future. These men are not dead for us. In the renewed life to be introduced amongst us in this place we shall walk and be guided in the light of their example, our souls shall be enriched in the inheritance of their virtues—the richest patrimony they could leave to their descendants of the cloister. We shall be aided, in our approaching difficulties, by the efficacy of their intercession, for each of them rising in spirit before me from these newly-blessed foundations, as the apparition of Jeremiah the prophet came up before the High Priest Onias, seemeth in the passing vision, 'as a man admirable for age and glory, and environed with great beauty and majesty'; each is to us in the hour of coming regeneration for our altars and country as the prophet was to the priests and people of Israel, 'a lover of his brethren and of the people of Israel—one that prayeth much for the people, and for all the Holy City.' It is, I fear not to avow it openly, that the religious spirit of such old friars, and of many like them, whose bones lie buried and dishonoured under the vast unsightly modern ruins on Crosse's Green, once St. Mary's Isle, may be brought back and dwell amongst us, the inheritors of their profession and ministry—it is for this purpose that our present community has laid this day the foundations of a convent which is to arise amidst countless discouragements, 'in straitness of times,' such as those recorded in Holy Writ, when the second Temple was to be restored after the Captivity. No matter, we must not be discouraged in undertaking so arduous but so glorious a work.

" Neither shall we curtail its proportions, or clip its beauty of design. The destination of a convent intended for Dominicans, whose profession as friars preachers embraces the seclusion and asceticism of the cloistered monk with the missionary zeal and cultivated talents of the apostolic priest, should be impressed on the very character and plan of its architecture—that architecture shall be what is called Romanesque. It at once sufficiently harmonizes with the more classical Roman order prevalent in the adjoining temple; and is, moreover—a consideration not to be overlooked—national, as it is but a revival of that more ancient than the Gothic style, which yet may be seen in many of our oldest ecclesiastical edifices built in the country, when Ireland was famed amongst the nations as 'the island of saints and scholars.' You may trace our design in the outline foreshadowed in the foundations just risen from the rock. Here, in this western end, are to be the great rooms for general use—the spacious library, so indispensable for priests, whose ministry requires assiduous study and extensive as well as profound learning; there is to be the oratory, where the religious may retire betimes to pray, and at the canonical hours to recite together the divine office; further is to be the chapter room, where the assembled brethren may be trained and perfected in the spirit and practice of their rules and constitutions by seasonable monition and mutual edification and encouragement; and here, too, is to be the extensive schoolroom, once a necessary portion of every Dominican convent, that was called a 'house of studies.' In the midst, projecting forward in that angle of the building, the abbey tower shall arise, with its glittering cross on the summit, to be hailed from afar by the homeward traveller and the devout pilgrim; and in its highest story shall be the bell chamber whence shall issue forth thrice every day the sweet sounds of the 'Angelus,' and the frequent summons for priests and people, to remind all of the approaching hour of sacrifice and prayer ; and there, too, shall be the muniment room for the archives of the Dominican Order in Ireland. In the eastern and main portion of the house you can already trace the cells of the friars of the convent ranged along the corridors, in beautiful but simple symmetry at either side, all of moderate size, but of exactly uniform proportions, thus showing forth in the very details of architectural arrangement 'how good and how pleasant it is for brethren to dwell together in unity.'

"Some of my friends have asked, since we came on the ground, why is not your convent planned more like a commodious ordinary dwelling house ? why laid out on so large a scale ? why constructed with such massive masonry ? ' As I am now publicly addressing you all, I may, from this place, remind my enquiring or remonstrating friends that the founders of Catholic establishments, such as our projected convent, can never divest their minds of a belief in the promised immutability and visible splendour of their Church, and that the nearer our religious institutions approach, in the very durability of their materials and the beauty of their construction, to the imperishable and glorious type of religion itself, the more clearly and unmistakably we show forth the depth and solidity of our Catholic faith and earnestness. As long, therefore, as St. Mary's temple, which rests in its grandeur on the rock beneath our feet, shall withstand the shocks of future time, so enduring, I think, should be its indispensable appendage—the house now founded for the officiating ministry of its altars, confessionals, and pulpits. A religious house should not be modelled according to the narrowness and low level of our modern prejudices, but, as near as the altered circumstances of the age and country will permit, after the form of the ancient abbeys still so strong and beautiful even in the ruins which persecution rather than time effected. A religious house, while suited to the exigencies of the present, should be designed and laid down with reference to the probabilities of the future, though its progress towards completion may be interrupted and retarded by unexpected casualties, and should be prudently regulated by the extent of actual and available resources. Catholicism in these countries is at present in a state of transition, not from civil persecution to political ascendancy, but from the most abject state of servitude to the fullest liberty ; and may not time, therefore, develop at no distant period opportunities of increasing the number and efficiency of our present small and, considering the claims of religion upon us, inadequate conventual family ? A time, too, may come—and sooner perhaps than is apprehended—when, on the suppression or decay of our collegiate establishments abroad, to which the penal laws of former times had exiled our students, the education of our young clergymen must be conducted by learned professors at home ; and, I ask, would not the citizens of Cork rejoice that St. Mary's church and convent and college should cluster, as the gems on a mural crown, upon the summit of this rock upon which we are now assembled ; and, while gleaming on the sunny declivity of this hill, should be seen from the principal streets and bridges of this city, and from the whole circuit of its beautiful and far-famed environs. And though all the cells spread out on the general plan may not instantly be needed for the monastic and educational purposes I have just indicated, how desirable it would be that the pious and hard-worked priests of the mission, in this and the neighbouring dioceses, should have an opportunity presented in a religious house such as, with God's blessing, this shall be, to repose occasionally from the labours and distracting cares of parochial duties, and refresh and strengthen their toil-worn spirits in the delicious exercises of a spiritual retreat. And oh ! that all these cells were at this moment finished, how gladly, as Abraham received into his tent the angel visitors, would not the Dominicans of Cork throw wide the gates of their convent for as many as could be accommodated with hospitable shelter, to the ill-treated exiled sons of St. Ignatius who might reach our southern shores ! Welcomed should be the persecuted fathers of that illustrious order of missionaries and scholars, which, by special ordinance of our constitutions, we are bound to revere with singular honour, and to cherish with fraternal predilection.

"But I must trespass no longer on the too considerate indulgence of my friends. Again, my lord, I thank your lordship for myself and for my brethren; may the vows and suffrages of your people and clergy be heard for your long and peaceful life, and may all the desires with which your paternal heart is overflowing, for the instruction and sanctification of your numerous flock, be realised; may we, your lordship's clergy, secular and regular, be, emulous only to do good, fellow-labourers for the perfecting of the saints, for the work of the 'ministry, for the building up of the body of Christ, but ever doing the truth in charity, that we may in all things grow up in Him who is the Head.' For the accomplishment of the work before us I have no fears. No doubt difficulties foreseen and unexpected shall be encountered, and with God's blessing shall also be overcome. True, large funds are required, but the whole building need not be finished at once; it can be done in such parts as may be required, and as resources may be supplied. At worst, it is a work of time. The penny of the poor man will be as ungrudgingly given as the sovereign of the richer neighbour. If the clergymen of our house had not given to the citizens of Cork, and generations yet to come, several hundreds of pounds, the joint contributions of their Order, towards the erection of St. Mary's Church, we should not be necessitated now to apply to the public for much assistance towards the building of St. Mary's Priory. On our parts, personally, it shall be a work of much toil and sacrifice, but yet sweet, because a labour of love, and hope, and regeneration. Why should we fear? Is not St. Mary our patroness, and will she 'despise our petitions in our necessities?' Is it not auspicious that our foundations are laid and blessed on the opening of the month of May, especially sacred to her devotion. Is it not God's work more than ours? The same Providence which supplied the means for erecting the grand church will erect for us this humble convent, and in its own good time will accomplish the designs and aspirations for the fulfilment of which we have this day, my Lord Bishop, invoked the episcopal blessing on this corner stone of the building. 'Unless the Lord build the house, they labour in vain who build it.'"

At the beginning of this year Father John A. Ryan, above-mentioned, was elected prior of St. Mary's, his election being confirmed by the Provincial, Father Dunne. He resigned after a few months, and was immediately succeeded by the Rev. B. T. Russell. [18] How well-deserved was this promotion can be fully understood when we remember that to Father Russell's zeal and untiring energy, aided by the faithful people of Cork and the Catholic laity of the United Kingdom, is almost wholly due the existence of St. Mary's church and priory.

The brethren who formed the community at that time were : Very Rev. B. T. Russell, prior ; Very Rev. J. P. Leahy, sub-prior ; Very Rev. J. A. Ryan, S.T.M. ; Very Rev. J. O'Connor, S.T.M., and Rev. Aaron L. Roche.

The annals of this house, published by Father Russell, and dating from the laying of the foundation stone, concludes with these significant words : " What God hath commenced, may He accomplish to the end." When we consider the time and circumstances under which the work was begun, we are surprised to find how successful was the result, as shown in the present residence, which though unassuming possesses much architectural beauty viewed in its various details.

[18] April 17th, 1848.

The building was commenced shortly after the famine of 1847, during which heart-rending crisis of our local history the priests of St. Mary's were amongst the foremost to alleviate the sufferings and attend to the spiritual wants of the people. Many instances might be quoted in which the prior and his brethren readily joined with their fellow-citizens in the grand work of charity, which, in such an appalling crisis, is incumbent on every man worthy the name of Christian. To this zeal and energy on the part of St. Mary's community is attributed in great measure the promptitude and willingness of the people of Cork, when disease and famine had passed away, in responding to the appeals made for funds to erect a suitable residence. The present priory is an enduring monument of their generosity, for rich and poor contributed most cheerfully to its construction. [19]

[19] We find by the annals of St. Mary's, that on the 12th May, 1848, the plot of ground adjoining Mulgrave Road, and measuring about 114 feet 5 inches, was purchased by the community from the Wide Street Commissioners for one hundred and fifty pounds, the names of the assignees being Francis Lyons, Danie Murphy, William Clery, William B. Hacket, and John O'Connell. Five days after the deed of transfer (kept in the Deposit of St. Mary's) was duly registered in Dublin. For the remainder of the site of church and priory the Fathers have to pay an annual rent of over one hundred pounds, which sum is generously contributed each year by the citizens.

Chapter IV.
Unexpected Blessings.

<pre>
For one thing only, Lord, dear Lord, I plead—
      Lead me aright ;
Though strength should falter, and though heart should
      bleed,
         Through Peace to Light.

I do not ask, Oh Lord, that thou shouldst shed
      Full radiance here ;
Give but a ray of peace, that I may tread
      Without a fear.
                                ADELAIDE A. PROCTER.
</pre>

N occurrence of great importance to the Dominicans of Cork took place on the 18th October, 1848. The bishop of the diocese, the Most Rev. Dr. Delany, examined and authenticated a number of Papal rescripts.[20] One of these refers to the body of St. Severus, martyr. His lordship, empowered by the Holy See, fixed for this saint's feast the 11th December, on which was granted a plenary indulgence, applicable to the souls in purgatory. To Dr. Hynes, O.P., a native of this city, the brethren owe the privilege of having this sacred

---

[20] These rescripts, which are in possession of the community, are dated 19th November, 1841, 14th and 21st February, 1842, S. Congregation of Indul., Rome.

relic. We are informed that his Eminence Cardinal Patrizi proceeded, by special order of Gregory XVI., to the cemetery of St. Agnes, in the Via Nomentana, and thence removed the body, which was handed over to Dr. Hynes, with power to dispose of it according to his own discretion. Permission was likewise granted to expose it to public veneration. Though the phial of congealed blood, the palm branch, and other tokens of martyrdom are sometimes found in the Roman cemeteries with the bodies of the martyrs, their names are not always discovered. In such cases the Sovereign Pontiff gives a name by which these saints are honoured by the faithful, but there was no such want with regard to St. Severus, for besides the phial tinged with blood, was the inscription, "Sebero in Pace." He is, therefore, venerated under the name received at baptism. On arrival of the body at the Custom House, Dublin, the case in which it was enclosed was opened in presence of three members of the Dominican Order, as we see by the following attestation :—

"We, the undersigned, testify that the case containing the body of St. Severus was opened in our presence to satisfy the officers of the Custom House that nothing was placed in or taken from it, and that it remained under our close inspection until it was closed with a red riband, and sealed in several places with the small seal of our Province. Dated this 24th day of June, 1842. Convent of St. Saviour's, Dublin.

     Br. William V. Harold, Provincial.
     Br. John Albert Ryan.
     Br. John P. Leahy."

When these precautions had been observed, the martyr's body was forwarded to its destination, and

DR. HYNES.

placed under the side altar of St. Mary's, where it still remains.[21]

[21] The rescript relative to the body of this saint bears date 14th February, 1842, is signed by his Eminence Cardinal Patrizi, V.-Gen. of the Pope, and countersigned by the Archbishop of Colossus, Vicegerent for the time being.

The other rescripts authenticated by the bishop (namely, that for the privileged high altar of St. Mary's, Pope's Quay, plenary indulgence on the anniversary of the blessing of the Church, and on that of deceased benefactors) were likewise obtained from the Pope by Dr. Hynes, who shortly after at the request of the Prior of St. Mary's, purchased for the church the beautiful picture of the "Ascension," which now adorns the sanctuary.[22]

As I am quite sure that their perusal will be interesting to many of our readers, I here give the leading facts of this distinguished prelate's career.

John Thomas Hynes received the Dominican habit at an early age in Lisbon, at the College of Corpo Santo. After some months he was removed to Rome, where by a special dispensation[23] he made his solemn profession in the church of Santa Prassede, then in the hands of the Irish Dominicans. Being ordained priest at the termination of his studies, he returned to Cork, and was assigned to the convent in Dominic Street. Father Hynes was subsequently appointed Bishop of Zante and Cephalonia, and then transferred to Demerara. We are told that he governed these dioceses with the greatest prudence, and was most assiduous and zealous in preaching the Word of God.

[22] When writing to the community relative to the above, Dr. Hynes made the following remark :—" Hogan and I had many consultations about your picture. This is the great Roman sculptor of the day, a Cork man, who did honour to his native country by the fame which he acquired in the city of artists."

[23] Canon Law requires that the year's Novitiate should be passed uninterruptedly in the same house.

Obliged through delicacy of health to relinquish the laborious duties of the Episcopal Office, he came back to his native country. He was accustomed at this time to spend some months of each year in the South of Europe. More than twenty years ago, when coming home, he was taken suddenly ill in Paris, where he died, fortified by all the consolations of religion. His remains were brought to Cork, and laid in St. Finbarr's cemetery. A beautiful monument marks the spot where he is buried.

On the 10th May, 1849, John G. Galwey, of Shandon Street, on behalf of the Very Rev. John O'Connor and the other Dominican fathers, entered into an agreement with Mr. James Willard, Pope's Quay, whereby the latter bound himself to construct a high altar of the form, dimensions, and material (Italian marble) of one executed by him and then in possession of the Rev. Father Daly, P.P., Kilmurry. This agreement was signed and witnessed by John Morrogh. The altar, erected in due time, though not pretentious, was still beautiful in its simplicity.[24] It was afterwards replaced by the present magnificent high altar designed by Mr. Goldie, of London, as were likewise the apse and baladchino erected at the same time. The former altar was subsequently removed to the church of St. Finbarr's West, built by the exertions of the late dean of Cork, the Right Rev. Monsignor Neville.

[24] It was consecrated by the Right Rev. Dr. Delany on the 10th June, 1851.

About the middle of September of this year, the Rev. James Joseph Carbery, O.P., returned to Ireland from Rome, where he had recently completed his studies at the Dominican College of San Clemente. He was assigned to the house of his affiliation at Newbridge. The members of the Cork community, remarking how great was the spirit of zeal which animated this young priest, begged of the Provincial to attach him to St. Mary's. The request was acceded to, and we soon find Father Carbery engaged in the active work of missionary life in Cork, where he became distinguished as a preacher. The Rev. John Thomas Willard, who in after years was so well known and loved by the people of Cork, returned to his native city towards the end of January of the following year, having completed his studies at the college of Corpo Santo, Lisbon, and was assigned to St. Mary's.

Early in August, 1850, the Most Rev. Dr. Cullen, Primate of All Ireland, invited the Dominican Provincial, the Very Rev. J. P. Leahy, to attend the National Synod which was to assemble on the 22nd in the Cathedral of Thurles. The profound learning and unaffected piety of this good priest was the subject of universal admiration at the Synod.

An event of the utmost concern, and of beneficial results to the Dominicans, occurred during this year. His Holiness Pius IX., after his return from Gaeta, where he had been exiled for well nigh eighteen months, appointed as Vicar-General of the Order the Rev. Alexander Vincent Jandel. The new Superior was born

FATHER JANDEL.

in Champsey, in France, on the 18th July, 1810, and was ordained priest at Metz on the 20th September, 1834. Meeting Lacordaire some three years subsequently,[25]

[25] Father Jandel was then Superior of the Petit Seminaire of Pont-de-Mousson.

the intellectual power of the great preacher made a deep impression upon him. He went to Rome in 1839, for the purpose of preaching the Lent at the church of San Luigi dei Francesi. At that time he had resolved to enter the Society of Jesus, but, acting on the advice of a priest of that Society, decided to become a Dominican, and accordingly received the habit of the Friars Preachers on the 13th May, 1841, in the convent of La Quercia,[26] from the hands of the Most Rev. Father Ancarani, then General of the Order. The year previous Lacordaire had made his solemn profession on the same sacred spot. The appointment of Father Jandel as Vicar-General was not in accordance with what is prescribed by the Constitutions of the Order, as a General Chapter should have been summoned for the purpose; but in the disturbed state of society, especially in Rome, it would not have been prudent for those entitled to vote to assemble in a body from the different provinces. Therefore the Holy Father, in the exercise of his supreme power, deemed it right to provide a head and pastor for this portion of Christ's flock, though he did not decide this important matter without having first consulted, through the Most Rev. Father Buttaoni, master of the Sacred Palace, Father Palmeggiani, under whose care the Rev. A. Jandel had made his novitiate. The choice of a Superior who had worn the Dominican habit for only ten years caused some surprise amongst the members of the Order ; but

[26] This means "The Oak." It is a sanctuary of the Madonna near Viterbo.

very soon was seen the wisdom of the selection, for Father Jandel by his learning and piety proved that it was the hand of God that marked him out for the position to which he was unexpectedly raised.

On account of the disturbed state of the times, and oft-recurring epidemics, some relaxation had crept into the Order; but that its members were still animated by the spirit of their founder was evident by the ready acquiescence with which they followed the advice of their saintly Vicar-General, who impressed upon them the necessity of the faithful observance of their rules. The Irish brethren, ever ready to listen not only to the commands but even to the wishes of their superiors, were amongst the first to submit to the directions which emanated from his wisdom and prudence. The members of the Cork community showed not the least hesitation in adopting every suggestion, and quite regardless of any sacrifice which such submission entailed they considered only their spiritual interests and those of the people frequenting their church.

The priorship of St. Mary's becoming vacant on the 17th April, 1851, the Rev. B. T. Russell was again chosen Superior. His election was willingly sanctioned by the Provincial. On the 20th July the Very Rev. Robert Augustine White made a visitation to St. Mary's, and in his report passed high eulogium on the fathers for their zeal and " regular observance," which, under the circumstances was singularly in accordance with the aspirations and wishes of their Vicar-General. Some few weeks subsequently the latter came in person to visit the community, still living in Dominick Street. His advent in Ireland was an honour which, according to the annalist of St. Mary's, had never since the time of St. Dominic been conferred on the *Hibernia Dominicana;* and his account, as recorded in the books of the Cork Convent, quite coincides with the views previously expressed by his Visitor-General. Father Jandel, who on this occasion was accompanied by Father White and Dr. Griffiths, O.P., bishop of the Cape of Good Hope, was waited on by Dr. Delany and other distinguished persons of the city. In his tour through England and Ireland he was shown the greatest reverence, though some ecclesiastical dignitaries did not approve of his wearing the habit in public when passing through these countries.

In the following month Mr. James Roche, who was truly called the "Roscoe" of our city, because of his vast literary attainments, wrote the following letter to Father Russell. As it refers to his admirable essays just then published, I consider its insertion here desirable.(27)

"National Bank of Ireland,
REV. DEAR SIR, Cork, 27th August, 1851.

You will please to accept from me for your community a copy of the *Essays*, of which, as the impression was very limited, not more than ten now remain unappropriated. Should you find leisure to look over them, pray indulgently recollect the writer's very many years, and very discordant general demand on his time. Some of them you probably have already seen, but here

---

(27) These essays by Mr. Roche are to be found in the Cork Library, also in that of St. Mary's.

they are all considerably enlarged and corrected. The press compositor's constant sickness has caused many errors still apparent, though marked for amendment in the proofs on every occasion by me, through the stupidity of the under-workmen, and sometimes, too, from their assuming a right to alter what they deemed wrong. Thus, Campbell's line in the *Pleasures of Hope*, 'Like angels' visits, few and far between,' was by these mercenary gentlemen ascribed to Moore's *Lalla Rookh*, which like blunders did not reach me until too late to correct.

Believe me, Rev. Dear Sir,
Yours most respectfully,
JAMES ROCHE."

A second letter from Mr. Roche to Father Russell (who had sent him a copy of his abridged *Annals of St. Mary's of the Isle*, with an account of the new Priory) contained the subjoined interesting information :—

"I have read with pleasure the *Account of the New Dominican Convent, etc.*, which you were so good as to present me. I perfectly recollect Dr. Nugent, who in 1784 or 5 accompanied the late Standish Barry, of Leamlara, to France, and remained with him for about a year at Nancy, in Lorraine. I do well remember seeing Father John Sheehan at Louvain in 1793, when the late Joseph Oliffe, the bishop's[28] father, was a student there. It was there that my brother Richard of your Order said his first Mass, 17th March, St. Patrick's Day, 1778. He had declined the offer of an uncle, then one of the first merchants in Rotterdam, to make him his partner and heir, a sacrifice of forty thousand pounds thus perfected, rather than abandon his vocation. This large sum afterwards devolved to the family in general, my uncle having died intestate."[29]

---

[28] Dr. Oliffe, O.P., of Madras, is the prelate here alluded to.

[29] The originals of these letters are kept in the deposit of St. Mary's.

On the 22nd October, 1851, the Very Rev. R. A. White sent to the Dominican communities of Ireland a memorable document, dated from St. Saviour's, Dublin, in which he laid down certain ordinances in accordance with the missionary state of the country, and suitable to the number of priests considerably reduced by religious persecutions. In January of the following year the Rev. B. H. Power[30] was affiliated to St. Mary's. He was a young priest of rare culture and intelligence, being remarkable for his musical and literary abilities.

About this time the prior wrote to Dr. Newman to express his sympathy with the distinguished Oratorian on the occasion of the well-known action brought against him by the infamous apostate Achilli. He received the following reply :—

"Oratory, Birmingham,
Jan. 17th, 1852.

MY DEAR FATHER,

Your kind and satisfactory letter came to-day, and I am obliged to you for it. It is a great consolation to me to hear of your good prayers for me. I know the value of them, and feel very grateful. Good will come of it if I am so supported. Achilli has just shown the white feather, though it involves a very anxious crisis. He is attempting to hinder me from bringing any witness to court, by going off on some technical objection.

Yours, my dear Father Russell,
Very truly in Christ,
JOHN H. NEWMAN, of the Oratory."

---

[30] A nephew of the Very Rev. B. T. Russell, O.P., and educated at Corpo Santo, Lisbon.

On the 5th of the following month Father Russell went to St. Saviour's, Dublin, to replace the Rev. Augustine White, prior, who, having been appointed assistant to the General of the Order, was obliged to take up his abode *pro tem.* in the Hospice of the Minerva, the official residence of the General. On the day of Father Russell's departure, a meeting of the community was held to consider a proposal made by a committee of the butter merchants of the city for the purchase of the old house in Dominick Street. The Priory, Pope's Quay, was then nearly finished, and the committee being desirous of building a market on the site, Father Russell agreed to transfer the interest for a certain monetary consideration. [31]

On the 3rd June, 1852, the Dominicans took possession of their new home, and as Father Russell's desire was that those who aided him should never be forgotten by the community he instituted the custom of offering the twelve o'clock Mass every Sunday of the year for the welfare of all benefactors, living and dead.

At a chapter held in the College of Newbridge on the 3rd of the following month, the Rev. B. T. Russell was elected Provincial. With the least possible delay the Cork community assembled and unanimously chose

[31] This money was expended in liquidating the debt on the Priory. The plot of ground formerly called the Strand, fronting Pope's Quay, containing about seventy-five feet, then in the tenancy of the Rev. B. T. Russell and Rev. J. Leahy, was granted to the former by the Commissioners of the Encumbered Estates Court, Mountifort Longfield and Charles James Hargrave, on the 24th March, 1852. The deed, which was duly signed in Dublin, is kept in the deposit of St. Mary's.

the Rev. J. P. Leahy, S.T.M., [32] as prior. Some days previously the brethren received from the Vicar-General a circular letter relating to the important subject of the studies of the Order. He informed them that the Pope had appointed a special commission to prescribe rules for Dominican studies suitable to the necessities of the present time. " In order," he says, " to meet the objections of the adversaries of religion, we must not only have a thorough knowledge of the teaching of St. Thomas, our trusted leader, whose principles—philosophical and theological—we are by a happy necessity bound to follow, but we must likewise be grounded in the admitted experiments of modern science, as otherwise we should be like soldiers, who in the days of gunpowder invention have recourse only to the shield and arrow to repel the attack of the invader. Again, before studying the ' Summa,' we should strive to become well versed in controversy, especially in matters in which the infidelity of our own times endeavours to mislead and contradict the principles of true religion and morality. The Holy Scriptures and ecclesiastical history should be the subjects of our anxious application, and in order to succeed in acquiring a proper understanding of the former, we should study the Hebrew and Greek languages." Meanwhile, to show the necessity of the greatest care in the selection of books, and in confirmation of his wisdom in prohibiting students to read

[32] Ex-Provincial.

a certain class of works, Father Jandel quotes the inspired words of St. Paul—" See that no one be deceived by philosophy or foolish falsehood according to the tradition of men, according to the elements of the world, and not according to Christ." The Vicar-General, who like St. Dominic was enthusiastic about the grand teaching of St. Paul, closes his letter with the words of the Apostle to Timothy—" Keep that which is committed to thy trust, avoiding the profane novelties of words. . . attend unto reading, to exhortation, and to doctrine. . . . meditate upon these things, that thy profiting may be manifest to all "—1st Epistle, chapters iv. and vi. [33]

[33] The resolutions approved of by the Papal Commission, and mentioned in this circular, were incorporated in the constitutions of the Order, and are to be found in the new edition, page 537, No. 1061, and following.

Chapter V.
A Succession of Joys and Sorrows.

> He who sent them fishing is with them still,
>   And He bids them cast their net;
> And He has the power their boat to fill,
>   So we know He will do it yet.
>
> Though the storm is loud, and our voice is drowned,
>   By the roar of the wind and sea;
> We know that more terrible tempests found
>   Their Ruler, O Lord, in Thee.
>
> ADELAIDE A. PROCTER.

ON the 29th May, 1852, the Rev. John Albert Ryan, S.T.M., was called to his reward, in the seventy-eighth year of his age. The bishop, Dr. Delany, officiated at the funeral obsequies, assisted by the Right Rev. Dr. Hughes, O.S.F., Vicar Apostolic of Gibraltar, and a large number of the local clergy. His remains were laid in the cemetery attached to the church. Father Ryan's career was varied and distinguished. As early as the year 1810, he delivered, in the South Parish Church, the funeral oration of the Right Rev. Florence McCarthy, coadjutor in the See of Cork. This discourse was afterwards published in pamphlet form, proving thereby that even then his eloquence was of no mean order. For some years Fathers Ryan

and Harold (a fellow Dominican, and subsequently Provincial of Ireland) conducted a boarding school at Bloomfield, in the neighbourhood of Dublin.[34]

REV. JOHN ALBERT RYAN, S.T.M.

Amongst its distinguished pupils was John Pius Leahy, late bishop of Dromore.

In the year 1815 an important historic event took

[34] This school was closed in the year 1815.

place in the old Townsend Street Chapel, Dublin. Five bishops were consecrated at the same time, and Father Ryan, whose fame as a pulpit orator had spread throughout Ireland, was invited to preach. In addressing the newly-consecrated prelates, he advised them against being swayed by the voice of the people where faith and morals were concerned, but rather to be to their respective flocks prudent leaders of thought, in order to guard them against the quicksands into which political bias and opinions might lead them. Some years afterwards, Father Ryan was appointed rector of the Dominican college of Corpo Santo, Lisbon,[35] but soon after, at the request of the Propaganda, he undertook a mission to Philadelphia. Having been successful, he returned to Cork in the year 1829 or '30, and six years subsequently[36] was appointed visitor-general of the convent of St. Catherine of Sienna, in Drogheda—a proof of the esteem in which he was held by the authorities of the Order. He died, as already mentioned, in 1852.

On the 20th October of this year, a meeting of the young men of Cork was convened by Father J. P. Leahy in one of the long rooms attached to the church. He invited those assembled to inaugurate in their city a branch of the Young Men's Society founded in Limerick by Dean O'Brien. After five or six weeks,

[35] The patents for this appointment were dated 21st February, 1822, and were sent on the part of the General by the Rev. Joseph Velzi, then Procurator General, and subsequently Cardinal.

[36] January 18th, 1836.

during which similar meetings were frequently held, Father Leahy had the happiness of seeing this admirable society established in Cork.

About the month of September, 1854, a provincial synod of Leinster was held in the pro-cathedral, Dublin. The archbishop, Dr. Cullen, who presided, announced that he had received a communication from the Pope, through the Cardinal Prefect of Propaganda, directing him to make known to those assembled his desire that the old religious orders be invited to give missions throughout the country. The provincial, Father Russell, who was present, cheerfully acceded to the request, saying that he and his brethren would willingly undertake such missionary work, as they considered it within the sphere of action of the Friars Preachers. The bishop of Kerry, Dr. Moriarty, who had always entertained a personal regard for the order, immediately invited the Dominicans to give a mission in Tralee, which was most successful.

On the 8th of the same month Father Leahy was appointed coadjutor bishop of Dromore. He wrote from Dublin to the sub-prior of St. Mary's, announcing with regret his resignation of the priorship, because it was the first step towards separating himself from his brethren. His consecration took place in the church, Pope's Quay, on Rosary Sunday, October 1st. The primate, Dr. Dixon, officiated, assisted by Dr. Delany and Dr. Kilduff, bishop of Ardagh. There were likewise present the Archbishop of Dublin, and the Bishops of Cloyne, Kerry, and Raphoe, as well as many priests from various dioceses in Ireland. After the consecration, the high sheriff and other Catholics of the city presented the new bishop with an address expressive of their profound esteem, accompanied with a rich service of altar-plate and a purse containing three hundred sovereigns. On the following day he received from the Young Men's Society, and others frequenting the Dominican Church, similar addresses of congratulation, as well as valuable presents. Dr. Leahy was subsequently entertained at a banquet given at the Mansion House by the bishop and priests, who also presented an address, to which amongst other signatures is attached that of Father Mathew.[37] Being very beautiful both in style and sentiment, it is here subjoined.

"TO THE RIGHT REVEREND JOHN PIUS LEAHY, D.D., BISHOP OF AULON, AND COADJUTOR BISHOP OF DROMORE.

MY LORD,

We, the clergy of this city and diocese, cannot allow this occasion of your elevation to the Episcopacy to pass without expressing our deep feeling of regret at the prospect of your departure from amongst us, as well as of the love and veneration that we entertain for your exalted character.

During your mission of twenty years amongst us, the many opportunities we have enjoyed of appreciating your rare endowments have served only to endear you the more affectionately to the heart of every one amongst us. We have admired the fervour and emotion of that eloquence with which you preached God's Word in the pulpit; we have profited by the profound and varied erudition which you have uniformly displayed in our hall

[37] The original is preserved in St. Mary's Priory.

of conference. In the moments of social intercourse you have attracted our regards by the unaffected gentleness and elegance of your demeanour. The engaging sweetness of your manner has encouraged us often to seek your counsel, and our confidence has been amply repaid by the soundness and wisdom of your advice. In the virtues that should adorn the priestly character you have ever been to us an example and a model. It is, therefore, my lord, with feelings of no ordinary regret that we contemplate our approaching separation.

The illustrious Order of Preachers, which was the ambition of your young heart and the choice of your ripened judgment, is graced by its chain of hallowed recollections in this your native city, as well as throughout the Church at large. Many of our holiest and distinguished predecessors in the ministry, who devoted themselves to the salvation of God's people—when the name of priest or friar was enough to bring peril or death, to immure them in the dungeon, or conduct them to the scaffold— were the children of St. Dominic. Many of the brightest ornaments of religion, whose memory will be ever enshrined in the hearts of the people, were members of the Order to which you belong. You have not fallen away from the virtues of your fathers in religion, and have proved yourself worthy of the name and habit you bear. What your own modesty would neither recognise or acknowledge has been now emphatically proclaimed in your selection, by the highest authority in God's church, for the august dignity of the episcopal office to which you have just been raised. We know full well, my lord, that the language of eulogy is distasteful to your good sense, and unwelcome to your ears. Your humility has ever sensitively shrunk from the faintest whisper of approbation or applause; you have been content to labour unobtrusively for God alone. But on this occasion, the eve of your departure, you will pardon our lingering with a fond remembrance on the noble and endearing traits of a character that we have so long and so deservedly revered. We hoped that for many a year to come it would be your lot, as it would be our delight, that you should continue to labour with us; but as God has ordained it otherwise, you have our warmest wishes and prayers for your future welfare. No length of time, no distance of place, shall sever the ties that bind us; and you will still permit us to claim you as a father and a friend. We derive some degree of consolation on your departure, from our conviction that your future career will be one of honour and of usefulness, that you will be an ornament to that venerable and glorious Hierarchy of Ireland to which you have been associated, and that your ministry, which we pray may be prolonged for many years, will be a source of happiness and blessing to the favoured flock that has been committed to your care:—

MICHAEL O'SULLIVAN, V.G.
DOMINIC MURPHY, V.G., P.P., St. Finbarr's.
EDMOND HOGAN, Provl. O.S.F.
JEREMIAH O'BRIEN, P.P.
GEORGE SHEEHAN, V.F.
JOHN F. FALVEY, P.P., Glanmire and Dunbullogue.
JAMES O'SULLIVAN, P.P., Blackrock.
DENIS F. MACLEOD, O.M.C.
PATRICK RIORDAN, R.C.V.
PATRICK A. LYONS, O.S.A.
AUGUSTINE MAGUIRE, R.C.C.
JAMES B. DALY, P.P., Kilmurry,
THEOBALD MATHEW.
JOHN JAS. MURPHY, Pres. SS. Peter et Paul.
WILLIAM CUNNINGHAM, R.C.C.
CHARLES O'CONNELL, R.C.C.
JOHN HOLLAND, P.P., Passage.
GEORGE BRENNAN, R.C.C.
TIMOTHY O'SULLIVAN, R.C.C.
TIMOTHY O'DONOVAN, P.P., Desertserges.
DENIS MACSWINEY, R.C.C.
DENIS MAHONY, R.C.C.
JOHN WALL, P.P., Watergrasshill.

PATRICK MURPHY, c.c.
PATRICK O'FLYNN, R.C.C.
CHRISTOPHER FREEMAN, R.C.C., Lower Glanmire.
DANIEL FOOTT, O.S.A.
PATRICK BEGLEY, R.C.C., St. Finbarr's.
EUGENE CULLEN, O.C.C.
CHARLES BROWNE, O.S.F.
DENIS O'DONOHUE, R.C.C.
J. BARRY.
JEREMIAH O'CONNELL, C.C.
JOHN KELEHER, P.P., V.F., Kinsale.
JOHN BROWNE, R.C.C.
SAMUEL LUCEY, P.P., Lower Glanmire.
JAMES J. O'REARDON, Provincial Capuchins.
JOHN MCNAMARA, R.C.C.
JOHN J. CROWE, C.C.
WILLIAM O'SULLIVAN, R.C., Vicar.
PATRICK MORAN, O.S.A.
MAURICE WALSH, P.P., Ovens.
THOMAS WALSH, R.C.C.
WALTER MURPHY, O.S.F.
THOMAS O'BRIEN, O.S.F.
JOHN P. CLANCY, R.C.C.
DANIEL HORGAN, P.P.
LAWRENCE GILLOOLY, C.M.
GEORGE A. HELY, O.S.A.

A grammar school was established about this time in St. Mary's for the education of postulants for the order, but was afterwards discontinued, the priory being made into a house of studies for those who were professed.[38] The school, however, produced excellent

[38] Father Bonello, a Maltese Dominican, was appointed Professor of Philosophy.

fruits, as four of the pupils joined the order—the present bishop of Cork, and the ex-provincial, Very Rev. Father Condon, being of the number. John Windele, son of the celebrated Cork archæologist, likewise attended this school. He possessed many brilliant qualities, which augured well for his future career, but died ere his hopes could be realized.

The following letter shows the special and affectionate regard which the General of the Order entertained for the community of St. Mary's.

"ROME, 10*th February*, 1855.

To the Very Rev. Prior and Rev. Fathers of the Convent, Cork.

MY DEAR REV. FATHERS,

Divine Providence has honoured your convent in a special manner, by calling, within the lapse of three years, one of its members to the government of the Province of Ireland,[39] and another to the sublime dignity of the Episcopate. The honour conferred on these two religious is a just recompense of their merit and zeal, and shows the high esteem in which your convent is held, whilst imposing upon you great obligations. It is your duty to sustain this reputation, and, by your devotion and generosity, to correspond to the call of God, to the desires of the Church, and to the favours already received.

Dr. Leahy and the Very Rev. Father Provincial have laboured strenuously in the erection of your convent. Consumed with the desire of re-establishing strict discipline, they have, by the choice of a convenient site, and the laying down of appropriate foundations, neglected nothing that might facilitate its accomplishment. When, four years ago, I had the pleasure of visiting

[39] Father Russell, who was elected Provincial July 3rd, 1852.

you, the house in Cork was the only one in Ireland which combined the form of a convent and monastic building. Now that you enjoy the results of these labours, you should strive to inherit the spirit which has inspired them, and to realise the object for which they were intended. I have too much confidence in your good will not to be persuaded that you will receive with joy this fatherly invitation, and that you will forthwith put it into practice by establishing in your community common life and observance. Your convent will thus become a model, and can, if necessary, be chosen as a Noviciate or House of Studies. It will especially encourage the young people who are at present being trained here in "regular observance," and who, on returning to their native country, will undoubtedly persevere in the same course.

If, owing to the small number of Religious and the multiplicity of your occupations, certain points of "observance" seem to you impossible, you have only to let me know, and I shall readily dispense you according to your necessity, and with the concurrence of the Provincial, until circumstances render them practicable, for I have no desire to impose on you an insupportable burden. I therefore appeal to your good-will, upon which I count, and in which I shall not be disappointed, and beg of our Lord to bless you. I also ask the assistance of your prayers for me and for the Order.

BR. A. V. JANDEL."

The Rev. Thomas R. Hyland[40] was, with four others, solemnly professed on the 11th February, 1855, in St. Mary's, Tallaght; Father Burke, who was then Master of Novices, presented them to the Provincial, who received their vows.

---

[40] Subsequently chronicler of the Cork house, and later on coadjutor bishop of Trinidad.

On the 3rd October, 1857, the Rev. Bartholomew Power, O.P.,[41] sailed for Australia, for the benefit of his health. Before his departure the citizens of Cork presented him with an address and one hundred sovereigns to defray expenses. The Rev. John O'Conner died on the 10th June, 1858, in the seventy-eighth year of his age, and was buried in the cemetery beside the remains of his confrere, Father Ryan. The Right Rev. Dr. Delany, and a large number of priests, assisted at the funeral obsequies. He was remarkable for zeal and eloquence.

As the front of St. Mary's Church had not been finished, the community decided to erect a portico. In order to further this intention, a public and most influential meeting of the citizens was held in the month of October, 1858. Daniel Donegan, J.P., presided, the secretaries being Timothy Mahony, J.P., and John George McCarthy, president of the Young Men's Society. Among those present were :—Messrs. William Fagan, M.P.; John N. Murphy, D.L.; David Leahy Arthur, J.P.; Nicholas D. Murphy, Edmund Burke, Michael Cagney, Michael McNamara, J.P.; Thomas Lyons, J.P.; James Murphy, Ringmahon; James J. Murphy, Denis O'Connor, M.D.; Maurice Murray; James, William, and Patrick Hegarty (brothers), etc., as well as the Prior and Sub-Prior of St. Mary's, with Fathers Willard and Costello, O.P. A collection list was opened, and the amount realized over £1,900.

(41) Ten years subsequently he died in the Antipodes.

In January, 1860, Father Carbery was elected prior of St. Saviour's, Limerick. The news of his removal was received with dismay by the people of Cork. In their desire to keep him amongst them, they petitioned the Provincial to leave him at St. Mary's, but Father White, owing to the duties of his office, could not accede to their wishes, and accordingly appointed Father Carbery to the important position for which he was so eminently qualified. On his departure he received a testimonial and public address from the citizens expressing their gratitude for his untiring zeal and marvellous energy in the promotion of their spiritual and temporal welfare.[42]

In September, 1861, the interior of St. Mary's was materially changed. The church was divided into nave and aisle (its present form), and the second communion rail, which caused a distinction of classes, removed.[43] The statue of our Lady, surmounting the portico was formally blessed and raised to its present position in the following December.[44] This statue was executed by Mr. Cahill, of Dublin, one of Hogan's most celebrated pupils, and is a copy of that erected by Pius IX. in the Piazza di Spagna, Rome,

---

[42] A deputation of the Guild of St. Thomas Aquinas, of the Cork Young Men's Society, had two years before this, on the 3rd January, 1858, presented Father Carbery with an address and silver-gilt chalice and patena.

[43] The architect engaged for this work was Mr. J. Hurley, of Cork. Gas was introduced into the church in 1855.

[44] The portico was erected a short time previously.

to commemorate the definition of the Immaculate Conception, on the 8th December, 1854.

The Rev. Joseph Dominick Fitzgerald, O.P., died on the 11th October, 1862, at the early age of thirty-seven years, after a long illness borne with exemplary patience and resignation. Having spent the first years of his priesthood in Demerara (West Indies), his health became seriously impaired. He returned to his native country in 1858, and was assigned to the convent of St. Mary Magdalen, in Drogheda. Some months before his death he went to England for change of air, but growing worse, he came to St. Mary's, Cork. where he departed this life surrounded by his brethren,

On the 16th July, 1863, the community was again favoured with a visit from their General, the Most Rev. Alexander Vincent Jandel. He was received with the utmost enthusiasm, even by the citizens, who thronged to the Church in great numbers, whilst the sacred edifice resounded with the anthems of welcome poured forth from the organ, and the priory bell pealed its most gladsome tones. Father Jandel remained two days in Cork, and then left for Limerick, accompanied by Father Willard. The latter was succeeded in the Priorship by Father Conway, during whose absence in Rome the Rev. W. D. O'Carroll, subsequently Provincial of the United States, and coadjutor bishop of Trinidad, was appointed vicar.

After Father Conway's return, the well-known appeal case, Simms *versus* Quinlan, was brought on for hearing before the Master of the Rolls. Two legacies of £500 each were bequeathed by Michael John Simms to the Rev. Fathers Conway, White, and Russell, for the improvement of St. Mary's, Church, and the education of two Dominican students respectively. These bequests had been set aside on the 13th January, 1864, by Mr. William Brooks, Master in Chancery, and his decision was confirmed by the Master of the Rolls on the 4th November, the legacies thereby reverting to the residuary legatee.

The following protest was afterward published by the Very Rev. B. T. Russell :—

"In addressing my fellow subjects on the present occasion, I am made to feel that, though I am a priest of their communion, I am not united with them in equality of law. *They* are emancipated, enjoying civil rights and privileges. *I am* a proscribed religious, living under an unrepealed penal code.[45] I yield to unavoidable necessity in appealing for sympathy and redress in consequence of a recent decision (Simms *v.* Quinlan) in the Irish Court of Chancery, which, to the injury of my religious brethren and myself, enforces penal clauses of the Catholic Relief Bill against the regular clergy.

The country had almost forgotten, until this judgment was delivered, that the Emancipation Act of 1829—which enables Catholic gentlemen to enter Parliament, sit on the judicial bench, and to compete for almost all other places of honour and emolument in the State—was an act of disfranchisement for all subjects who, however loyal and otherwise deserving, should dare thenceforward to exercise the rights of Christian conscience, by professing the observance of the Gospel counsels as reduced to a practical system in monastic life. I need scarcely remark that such a law of the British Legislature is anti-Christian in

[45] See *Historical Notice of Penal Laws against Roman Catholics*, by R. R. Madden, published in 1865, page 66.

principle—an ordinance of unmerited persecution—a dark stain on the character of Catholic liberties, and, as to any real effect of conscience, neither to be dreaded nor obeyed. Its enactments disturbed the state of tranquil security in which the clergy of the religious orders, after suffering courageously ages of persecution, had been exercising their ministry since the year 1793, when the Irish Parliament passed the famous Act of Religious Toleration for the Relief of Catholics of every description. Sir Robert (then Mr.) Peel, in his speech on the Catholic question, is reported to have said—'Since 1793 there was nothing in the law of Ireland to prevent the residence of Monastic Orders in that country.'

Great alarm was excited by the announcement of the restrictions against religious communities of men, which were said to form an integral portion of the proposed measure of Catholic Emancipation. Petitions in favour of the Regular Orders were signed by the bishops, priests, and people, against the obnoxious statutes, which were called in the language of the day—*Securities*. The members of the monastic bodies in Ireland sent a deputation to London—of which two distinguished prelates, the Most Rev. Dr. O'Connor, of this city, Augustinian, and the Most Rev. Dr. Leahy, of Dromore, Dominican, are still surviving—to watch after the interest of the Regulars during the passage of the Bill through both Houses of Parliament, and to protest in the name of their religious brethren against the violation of the freedom of conscience with which they were menaced.

To lull the apprehensions of the regular clergy, and silence popular complaints and remonstrances, the leaders of the party in favour of Emancipation, fearing lest the exceptions so generally taken to those penal provisions might obstruct or retard the immediate passing of the great boon for the Catholics of the empire, held out assurances that the section of the Bill for the eventual suppression of all monastic institutions in Ireland and Great Britain should remain a *dead letter* on the Statute Book, and in course of time should prove to be quite harmless. That hope is now found to be delusive.

The late important case(46) decided by the Irish Lord Chancellor has called up the *dead* law to life and vigour in all the malignity of its sectarian spirit, and all practical mischievousness of its letter. That hated and persecuting enactment has been employed to drag the venerated Priors of St. Saviour's, Dublin, and of St. Mary's, Cork, with myself, from our accustomed retirement into the public courts of law. A necessity was thus imposed upon our honour and conscience to vindicate, by the advocacy of eminent counsel, the pious Catholic intentions of a deceased friend, whom we still remember and respect in his grave, and to defend the sacred rights with which we were entrusted in the good man's will against an aggressive act of sacrilegious spoliation. Through the judgment pronounced in this case by the Chancellor, we have been deprived of means bequeathed to us by a lamented benefactor towards the maintenance of one of our principal places of worship, and also towards the endowment of the College of the Rosary for Home and Foreign Missions of our Order, which we are now endeavouring to erect at Tallaght, near Dublin, amidst many trying financial difficulties.

My object in addressing this statement to the Catholics of the Empire is to solicit, in a most respectful and earnest manner, contributions of pecuniary aid for the indemnification of our losses and the payment of heavy legal costs, all of which have been inflicted on the Very Rev. Fathers White, Conway, and myself. Surely Catholics have not yet obtained 'full and unqualified' emancipation as long as the members of the religious Orders of their Church are deprived of the protection of the laws of their country.

      B. T. RUSSELL, Prior Provincial of the Order
        of St. Dominic in Ireland.
St. Saviour's, 30, Rutland Square, W., Dublin,
  Feast of St. Thomas Aquinas, O.P.,
    7th March, 1865."

(46) A faithful account of this case is found in R. R. Madden's *Historical Notice of Penal Laws*, page 76.

A public meeting of the Catholics of the city was held in the Chamber of Commerce, on the 25th of April, to protest against the disabilities to which the Regulars of Ireland were unjustly subjected. A subscription list was opened to defray law expenses, and the people of Cork responded with their usual generosity, their example being followed by the Catholics of Dublin and other parts of Ireland, making a total of over £450. Of this sum £380 were subscribed by the people of Cork.

At a Provincial Chapter of the Irish Dominicans, held in the Church, Pope's Quay, on the 23rd June, 1866, the Rev. Father Conway was appointed to the important position of Master of Novices in Tallaght. He therefore resigned the priorship of St. Mary's in the following December, and was succeeded by the Rev. P. T. Mullins, who died some years ago, and whose character is best described by saying that he was a man of few words, yet possessed of great power of mind and rare virtue. The Rev. Richard Dominic Scanlan, O.P., a native of Cork, died at St. Mary's on Christmas Eve, 1867. He was beloved by his brothers in religion, as well as by many friends outside the Order. Being like his Master, "meek and humble of heart," it does not surprise us that like his Divine Master he drew the hearts of others to him. Office and high mass, at which the bishop and a large number of the clergy attended, were offered on the 26th, and his remains were laid in the Dominican cemetery.

After an absence of twenty years, the Rev. B. T. Russell came back to St. Mary's as Prior, in March, 1871. His return was hailed by the community with great satisfaction. He fell seriously ill in the following October, but through God's Providence his health was restored, and his valuable life prolonged for many years. It is a remarkable coincidence that two of the Fathers living at the Priory at this time were afterwards raised to the episcopate—Father Hyland, who was appointed coadjutor-bishop of Trinidad, and Father O'Callaghan, now the revered Bishop of Cork. The Rev. P. V. Flood, O.P., who in the previous year was removed from our city to Dundalk, is now Archbishop of Trinidad.

The solemn opening of the apse and chancel of St. Mary's Church, and the unveiling of the baldachino [47] took place on the 27th October, 1872. The Very Rev. P. T. Conway, who was elected Provincial of Ireland on the 22nd June, sang high mass, and the Very Rev. J. J. Carbery preached in the presence of the bishop, who presided. [48]

Shortly after this joyous celebration, the community received, in the subjoined letter, the sad news of the death of their General, the Most Rev. Father Jandel.

[47] To the generosity of two kind friends (husband and wife), whose names we are not at liberty to disclose, is due the erection of this baldachino, the woodwork of which was executed by Mr. John Fitzgerald of Cork.

[48] A lease of the ground on which the apse is built was obtained from the Corporation. Mr. Barry McMullen, builder, was entrusted with the work, and Mr. Goldie, of London, was the architect.

"San Clemente, Rome,
Dec. 12th '72.

My Dear Father Russell,

It is with the most profound grief I have to announce to you that our dearly loved and much revered Father General is no more. He died last night at half-past six o'clock. May his soul rest in peace.

Believe me,
Ever affectionately yours,
(In great haste.) Br. Joseph Mullooly."

On the following day high mass was offered for the repose of his soul, and was attended by a large number of priests and people, many of whom remembered his kind and genial manner on the two occasions when he visited St. Mary's. The irreparable loss sustained by the death of their General cannot be fully understood, except by the brethren of the Order, who can never hope to have a superior better suited for the position than was Father Jandel. He was succeeded as Vicar-General by the Most Rev. Father Joseph Maria San Vito.

Early in October, 1873, St. Mary's again became a house of studies.[49] Two Fathers, the Very Revs. J. T. Deely, and J. L. Hickey, who held the position of superior, resigned their office in order to teach at the Priory. Ten young ecclesiastics (some of whom have since died, whilst others now occupy important positions in the Order) were committed to their guidance and tuition.

[49] The studies were discontinued some years previously, when those who had made part of their philosophical or theological course went to Rome and elsewhere.

The sixth centenary of the angelic Doctor St. Thomas Aquinas was celebrated in March, 1874, with great pomp and devotion, in the Church, Pope's Quay. For three consecutive days high mass was solemnized, as likewise on the following Sunday, when the bishop, the Most Rev. Dr. Delany, presided, and the Rev. John Coughlan, of SS. Peter and Paul's Church, now the Ven. Archdeacon of the Diocese of Cork, delivered "a discourse," as the chronicler of St. Mary's described it, "highly finished and worthy of the occasion." Sermons were likewise preached on Wednesday, Thursday, and Friday previous, by the Rev. William Madden, (now in Australia), the Very Rev. J. L. Hickey, O.P.,[50] and Rev. R. A. Sheehan, since deservedly promoted to the episcopal See of Waterford. Needless to say their sermons were greatly appreciated by those who heard them.

In the following year Very Rev. P. T. Conway, Provincial, with Father Hyland as companion, went on a visitation to the College of Corpo Santo, Lisbon. They started from Kingstown on the 7th July, arriving at their destination on the 13th. Having completed the visitation they left for Ireland in the "Boyne," the magnificent steamship of the Royal Mail Company, which set sail on the 11th of August. Little did our travellers dream of the terrible disaster which was to befall the vessel ere many days had passed, and which placed their lives and those of the

[50] Recently elected Provincial of Ireland.

other passengers in such imminent danger, that nought but the interposition of Providence could have saved them. On arriving near the coast of France, the steamer suddenly struck on a reef of rocks, and as she became a complete wreck, the passengers and crew had barely time to take to the boats before she rolled over and sank. When the tide subsided the boats were anchored to one of the rocks, and in that position they remained until past midnight (the ship having struck at 7.30 p.m.) when another unexpected danger threatened to immerse them in the waves with their human freight numbering four hundred. A Norwegian bark in full sail was fast bearing down on them, when all raised a simultaneous cry to warn the captain of the approaching vessel to keep off, thus saving their lives a second time, and likewise bringing to their rescue a party of fishermen, who were apprised of their danger by a diver engaged on a wreck which had occurred there but three months before. The boats were safely piloted to the island of Molène, and on the following day, the Feast of the Assumption, the passengers of the ill-fated "Boyne" were transferred to Brest by the French Government, in a small warship named "D'Estaing."

The two Fathers arrived safely in Dublin, but had unfortunately lost in the wreck a number of precious relics which they received in Lisbon, and though sought for with the greatest diligence, have not since been discovered.

Towards the end of this month the Synod of Maynooth was held, and Father Conway was one of those who took part in the deliberations of that venerable assembly.

Chapter VI.
Great and Good Men.

"O wondrous is the lot of him who stands
   A Christian priest, within a Christian fane,
And binds with pure and consecrated hands,
   Round earth and heaven, a festal, flowery chain ;
Even as between the blue arch and the main,
   A circling western ring of golden light
Weds the two worlds, or as the sunny rain
   Of April makes the cloud unite,
Thus links the priest of God
   The dark world and the bright."

"The Priest's Work," DENIS FLORENCE MCCARTHY, *Ballads, Poems, and Lyrics*, 1850.

THE Episcopal Jubilee of Pius IX. was celebrated with great pomp in Rome on the 3rd June, 1877. The bishop and priests of Cork, desirous of participating in the universal joy of Christendom, decided on having the city illuminated, and some idea of the enthusiasm of the citizens might be formed from the following quotation :—[51]

"Nothing of its kind has ever been witnessed here that could be compared with the illuminations of last evening. All the trades that come into requisition on such occasions had their hands filled to overflowing. Nevertheless it was found impossible

---

[51] *Cork Examiner*, June 8th.

to execute more than half the orders in the city. Nature, too, was laid under contribution, and the quantity of green boughs, and even trees, that were gathered together would have made a respectable forest. The principal feature of this demonstration was its universality.

St. Mary's Church was one of the most picturesque and tastefully decorated buildings in the city. The Priory was adorned by flags of various colours, and all the windows were brightly illuminated. The coronet on the statue of Our Lady surmounting the church, and the pedestal, were aflame with gas jets. The portico was bedecked with flags. From this point a line of banners spanned the river. On one, which hung from the centre, were depicted the Papal Arms, and bearing the mottos, ' Gloria in Excelsis,' and ' Long live Pius IX.' On the right and left respectively were shields with the inscriptions, 'Signum Fidei' and 'Ireland and Italy.' On the river and along the quays were tar barrels. A band was in attendance throughout the evening."

Eight months after this imposing display the news of the Pope's death was flashed by telegraph to the ends of the earth. Pius IX. died on the 7th February, 1878, and as his Episcopal Jubilee was celebrated with every token of joy in the previous June, so was sorrow now everywhere manifested. Many were the heartfelt prayers offered for the soul of the deceased Pontiff. A solemn requiem mass was celebrated in St. Mary's Church. The sanctuary and apse were draped in black, and around the catafalque in the centre of the church, as in other parts of the sacred building, were suspended various shields descriptive of the principal events in the reign of His Holiness. On the eastern tower was likewise raised the Papal standard at half-mast. All the churches of the city continued to exhibit signs of mourning until the election of Leo XIII. as universal pastor of the Church and bishop of Rome. The new Pope was crowned on the 3rd March with as much solemnity as possible under the trying circumstances which then prevailed.

After an interval of seven years, during which the Dominicans were governed by a vicar-general, the Most Rev. Joseph Larocca succeeded Father Jandel as master-general of the Order. He was elected in October, 1879, and, like his predecessor, was gifted with the spirit of zeal and prudence.

The marble pulpit[52] in St. Mary's Church was inaugurated on the 30th May, 1880, the opening sermon being preached by the Most Rev. Dr. Fitzgerald, bishop of Ross, who made an eloquent appeal to his audience to aid in liquidating the debt (£500), most of which was realized by the members of the Confraternity of St. Thomas Aquinas, which is appropriately called the "Angelic Warfare." On its base are inscribed the following words in gilt letters:—
" In honour of St. Thomas of Aquin, their holy patron, this pulpit was erected by the exertions of the young men of the Sodality of the ' Angelic Warfare,' 1880."

Just a month after this ceremony, the priorship of St. Mary's being vacant, the Very Rev. Father Carbery, ex-provincial, was elected to the office. He was

[52] It was designed according to the Italian renaissance, a style which prevailed in Italy during the fourteenth and two succeeding centuries.

universally greeted on his return to Cork, as he was much beloved by all classes whilst previously living in the city.

MOST REV. DR. CARBERY, O.P.
(*Late Bishop of Hamilton, Canada.*)

This position he retained about two months, when he was summoned to Rome by the General, who appointed him his assistant. After three years residence in the Eternal City he was raised to the episcopal See of Hamilton, in Canada. Though he presided only four years over this diocese, he promoted in a wonderful manner the spread of religion and piety. No wonder then that he is affectionately remembered by the people whose spiritual interests he so well guarded. Dr. Carbery came to Cork towards the close of the year 1887 with the intention of visiting Rome on the occasion of the Papal Jubilee, but his health, already impaired, became gradually weaker, and he peacefully passed away on the 19th December of the same year. After office and high mass at St. Mary's his remains were transferred to Limerick, and laid under St. Saviour's Church, in the vault built according to his own design. The following sketch of his life will, I doubt not, be of interest to those who were acquainted with the deceased.

He was born in Westmeath in 1822, and made his preparatory studies in the seminary of Navan. When nineteen years of age he went to Rome, and entered the Dominican Order. Having completed his studies at San Clemente, he was ordained priest and returned to Ireland. The first sphere of his labours was St. Mary's, Pope's Quay, where, for over ten years, he exercised the duties of his sacred ministry. At the time of his death one of the local papers observed :—" Though many years have passed since he lived among the people of Cork, the memory of Father Carbery is still fresh in the minds of those who knew him, and the kindly demeanour and kindlier actions of the young Dominican are still cherished and fondly remembered."

Recognising his great worth, the Provincial appointed him prior of St. Saviour's, Limerick, where, as in Cork, he produced a lasting impression on the hearts of all with whom he came in contact. Young men especially were the objects of his untiring zeal, and there are many who ascribe to him their success, both in spiritual and temporal affairs. After some years he was elected Provincial. Then, as already stated, he became assistant to the General, and subsequently Bishop of Hamilton.

More than a passing notice in this account of the Dominicans is due to the Rev. Thomas Burke, who, though not a native of Cork, willingly identified himself with the work of his brethren at St. Mary's. He felt quite at home with the people and their priests, and whenever invited to preach amongst them responded, as he often remarked, "with real pleasure." He was ever ready to aid them not merely in saving their souls, but in building their churches and schools, as well as providing for those in need of temporal assistance.

He was born in Galway on the 8th of September, 1830, and at an early age attended a school conducted by Dr. O'Toole in his native city. Then, as afterwards, he was remarkable for great wit and an exuberance of mirth. When seventeen years old he entered the Dominican Order in Italy, making his solemn profession in Perugia on the 5th January, 1849. He subsequently received minor orders from the present Pope, then bishop of that diocese. After three years' course of studies at the College of Minerva, Rome, he was deputed by Father Jandel to orgaize the Novitiate for the English province in Woodchester, Gloucestershire. On Holy Saturday, 1853, after his arrival, he was ordained priest by the Right Rev. Dr. Burgess. He was sent to Tallaght in 1855 to superintend the Irish Novitiate, which had then been opened. This position he held for twelve years, when he was appointed prior of Saint Clements, Rome. Returning to Ireland in 1869 he was assigned to St. Saviour's, Dublin, and in 1872 chosen to be visitor-general to the Dominicans of America. Meanwhile his reputation as a preacher had spread, and in the United States he found a wide field for his eloquence. His victorious defence of Ireland's rights against the unjust attacks of James Anthony Froude, the unreliable English historian, caused the defamer to retire ignominiously.

Father Burke preached so successfully in America that the monetary results in connection with objects of religion and charity amounted to seventy or eighty thousand pounds. Notwithstanding the excitement and success of this tour, that yearning to return home—so common to Irishmen when far from their own country—took possession of him, and he was frequently heard to say, " I am obliged to admit I feel a little lonely."

His return to Ireland was the subject of an enthusiastic welcome. Priests and people joined in presenting him with an address on his arrival at Queenstown. After visiting Galway, his native city, he went to Tallaght, and when called out to preach throughout the country spared neither his physical or intellectual powers, but ever spent them ungrudgingly

REV. THOMAS BURKE, O.P.

in his Master's cause. He frequently declined episcopal and other ecclesiastical dignities, as he felt that his special calling was preaching the Word of God. Cardinal Cullen once proposed to get him appointed to a See in Canada, but Father Burke immediately manifested his sorrow in the following words : " Your Eminence, I don't know how I can have offended you that you should seek to humiliate me in this fashion. You would like me to go to Canada, to that wild, barbarous region, where I'll surely be frozen or starved to death before six months are over my head ? Oh ! your Eminence, think better of it and let me off this time." Suffice it to say the proposal was not repeated. He was also offered the bishopric of Galway, but to the personal knowledge of the writer, declined the honour, his dearest wish being to live and die a Friar Preacher.

When therefore his precious life was cut short at the early age of fifty-three, a thrill of sorrow was aroused amongst the people of Cork. He died at Tallaght, county Dublin, on the 2nd July, 1883. Eight days previously had he risen from his bed in order to plead the cause of the starving peasantry of Donegal, and he said to those assembled on the occasion : " Three times I took up my pen to say that I could not come to-day, and each time it fell from my hand as I heard the cry of the famished ones asking for bread." After the sermon [53] he returned to Tallaght exhausted and agonizing, and never preached more. His remains were laid in the cemetery of the convent, but were afterwards removed to a mortuary chapel in the memorial church built as a reminder of what he has done for " faith and fatherland."

[53] Preached in the Church of St. Francis Xavier, Gardiner street, Dublin, on Sunday, June 24th.

Thus ended the career of one of our greatest Dominicans, who never swerved from the path he had chosen until called by his Divine Master to his well-earned reward.

On account of his intimate connection with the Dominicans of Ireland, and especially those of Cork, I would ask my readers to dwell with me awhile on the distinguished career of our present bishop, the Most Rev. Dr. O'Callaghan. The South Parish claims to be his birthplace. He was born in 1839, and at an early age was placed under the care of the Christian Brothers of the North Monastery. Here were instilled into his mind not only the principles of piety but likewise those of profane learning, for which he manifested great aptitude. He afterwards attended a school at Sunday's Well, conducted by Mr. D. O'Connor, then received lessons in the classics from Mr. O'Sullivan, South Mall, from whence he passed to the grammar school of St. Mary's Priory. In 1857 he entered the noviciate at Tallaght, the Rev. Father Burke being then master of the novices. Having made his profession, he studied philosophy under the same gifted teacher, and then left for San Clemente, Rome. He attended the theological lectures delivered by a Dominican at the college of the Minerva, and was elevated to the priesthood in 1864. Returning to Ireland after twelve months he was assigned to the convent of Tallaght, where for six years he was employed in teaching. He then was sent to Cork, and contracted the smallpox, which raged in the city, in

1872, but after a long illness regained his usual health and vigour. In the following year he was appointed prior of the West Convent, which is situated in Claddagh, a poor though romantic spot in Galway. This position he held scarcely twelve months when he became superior of St. Catherine's, Newry. After five years he went to Rome, where the students of San Clemente were placed under his care.

The Rev. Father Mullooly dying about this time, Father O'Callaghan succeeded him as prior of the Irish Dominican College.[54] This position he occupied for some years, when in June, 1884, he was appointed coadjutor-bishop of Cork. His consecration took place on the Feast of SS. Peter and Paul, in the Church of San Clemente, which was splendidly decorated for the occasion. Cardinal Simeoni, prefect of the Propaganda, was celebrant, assisted by Monsignor Salua, O.P., commissary of the Holy Inquisition, and Dr. Kirby of the Irish College. Dr. O'Callaghan arrived in Cork on the 2nd August, and was enthusiastically received by the people. After the death of Dr. Delany, one of the most eminent bishops of this century, Dr. O'Callaghan, by right of succession, took possession of the diocese. In order to give some idea of what he has done since then, it is merely necessary to quote the words of the *Irish Catholic* of the 8th September, 1888 :—" To speak in

---

[54] Father Mullooly was deservedly considered a most distinguished antiquarian. He discovered the ancient (now the subterranean) Church of San Clemente.

MOST REV. DR. O'CALLAGHAN, O.P.
(Bishop of Cork.)

detail of Dr. O'Callaghan's services to the Church since he has been raised to the episcopate would be impossible within the limits at our disposal, but it is no exaggeration to say that his lordship has displayed, in the great sphere of duty to which he has been called, those characteristic virtues of humility, devotion, and self-abnegation, as well as of firmness, in every righteous cause, which have always rendered him the beloved of his brethren in religion, and the esteemed and revered friend of those beneath his sway." May God prolong his life to continue the glorious work in which he is engaged—*ad multos annos.*

About three months after Dr. O'Callaghan's consecration, the Most Rev. Dr. Hyland closed his earthly career. As my readers may remember he was especially connected with St. Mary's. His death occurred at Trinidad, at the early age of forty-seven, but though his life was short it was full of merit and good works. He was born in Dublin in 1837, of a pious family, four members of which entered the religious state.[55] The deceased prelate joined the Dominican Order in 1856, and, like the bishop of Cork, made his noviciate at Tallaght, under the care of Father Burke. Having been professed, he went to Rome to complete his studies, to which he applied himself with assiduity and marked success. In 1861 he was raised to the priesthood, and returning to

---

[55] His brother, the Very Rev. Clement Hyland, O.S.F., was guardian of the convent of his Order at the time of the bishop's death, and two sisters had become " Poor Clares."

Ireland in the following year, was assigned to Holy Cross Abbey, Tralee, whence after twelve months he came to Cork. There are still in our city so many

MOST REV. DR. HYLAND, O.P.
(*Late Coadjutor-Bishop of Port of Spain.*)

friends by whom he is remembered that it is unnecessary to dwell at length on the qualities which distinguished Father Hyland. His zeal, eloquence, and self-sacrifice in the exercise of his sacred office are proverbial. During his stay in Cork he not only worked for the welfare of the people, but was likewise employed in teaching the students of St. Mary's, and meanwhile archivist of the convent.[56] The fruits of his energy in this interesting sphere have been such as to considerably lighten the labours necessarily entailed on the writer of this historical account.

For eighteen years Father Hyland thus devoted himself to the interests of religion, and was then deservedly promoted to the priorship of Tralee. Two years subsequently he was appointed coadjutor of the Most Rev. Dr. Gonin, O.P., archbishop of Trinidad. His consecration took place in the church of San Clemente, Rome, on the 30th April, 1882,[57] the celebrant being his Eminence Cardinal McCabe, the late archbishop of Dublin. He then went without delay to Port of Spain, where he literally wore himself out in the service of his Divine Master, and after two years died from the effects of a virulent climatic fever, his constitution, already enfeebled, being unable to cope with the disease. May his memory be cherished, and may his noble example ever live in the minds of his brethren and his numerous friends.

At the close of the visitation in June, 1885, the Very Rev. J. T. Towers, provincial, made the following observations :—" Since the last visitation the province,

---

[56] The writer succeeded to this office in November, 1890.
[57] The title assumed by him was that of Bishop of "Evrea."

and this house in particular, have had to lament the death of the Very Rev. Father Willard. The greater part of his holy life was spent in St. Mary's, of which he was a son. Here he edified his brethren by his sanctity, zeal, and self-sacrifice. Stricken down in the prime of life by a painful malady, he bore his trial with patience and resignation, so that when summoned hence his death was like his life, " precious in the sight of the Lord."[58]

His sterling qualities were so much appreciated that he was several times elected to the responsible position of prior, both in Cork and Newry. He died September 28th, 1884, aged fifty-eight years. His remains were laid in St. Mary's Cemetery.

On the 4th February, 1890, the Most Rev. Dr. Flood, O.P., was invested with the pallium as archbishop of Port of Spain. The ceremony took place in the cathedral of Trinidad, the Most Rev. Dr. Butler, S.J., bishop of Demerara, officiating. Amongst the many distinguished persons present was the Governor of Trinidad.

Dr. Flood has laboured strenuously for the welfare of those committed to his care. The grand results which have attended his untiring efforts do not surprise us when we consider the high qualities of mind and heart with which he is endowed. We wish him many

---

[58] A reference was likewise made to the new high altar, at the erection of which the baldachino was raised to its present height. This altar was consecrated by the Most Rev. Dr. O'Callaghan, on the 1st May, 1888.

years of happiness and success in the good work in which he is engaged.⁽⁵⁹⁾

The Very Rev. B. T. Russell, whose name is well known to our readers, died on the 10th July, 1890, in the Dominican Priory, Cork. His career was most distinguished. For seventy-four years he shone as a leader and an ornament in the Order to which he belonged. Bearing an extraordinary love to the habit of St. Dominic, and desirous of spending his life as an humble friar, he could not be induced to accept the episcopal dignity. The personal friend of many great men, he never aspired to other title than that of " Friar Preacher."

He was born in Cork, on the 25th March, 1799, and entered the Order when eighteen years old. Having finished his studies in Corpo Santo, he returned in 1823 to his native city, where, heedless of contempt and prejudice, which in those days was frequently the portion of priest and friar, he preached and laboured unceasingly in the old chapel of Dominick Street.

When Catholic Emancipation was granted to Ireland in 1829, our "silver tongued preacher," as he was called, making an appeal on behalf the Christian Brothers' Schools, thrilled his audience by the following expressive words :—" Let us give glory to God to-day, for to-day we are free ; our bonds have been broken, and we are delivered ; but no ! we are not *all* free. There

---

⁽⁵⁹⁾ The name of Father Vincent Flood is mentioned in the Records of St. Mary's Priory early in the year 1870.

is one slave in your midst, and that is he who addresses you. Yes, my brethren, yes. I, alas! am still a slave,

MOST REV. DR. FLOOD, O.P.
(*Archbishop of Port of Spain.*)

for I am still in the eyes of the law a felon."[60] This feeling of slavery did not however deter him from

[60] Father Russell alluded here to the exclusion of the regular clergy from the benefits of Catholic Emancipation. See his appeal on this subject, page 65.

exercising his ministry in pulpit and confessional during his long and laborious life.

His uprightness of character, blended with sweetness and discretion, as well as deep-seated piety, attracted not only the young, but those advanced in years. His Order was to him as poverty to St. Francis of Assysium, "his spouse and his queen." He lived only for its advancement, and his heart seemed to throb only for its welfare. We need but look on St. Mary's, its church and priory, both built by him, which are ornaments to the city, and, we trust, fountains of good—spiritual and temporal—to glean some idea of Father Russell's capabilities and well-regulated zeal. His peaceful, happy death was a fitting close to a life so full of merit and good works. He was buried in St. Mary's Cemetery after the requiem high mass, celebrated by the Most Rev. Dr. O'Callaghan, O.P. His brethren united with other dear friends of the laity in raising a beautiful monument in the sanctuary of the church, as a testimony of their sincere regard.[61]

Two months had scarcely passed, after Father Russell's demise, when Dr. Leahy, bishop of Dromore, departed this life. These distinguished men were fellow-students in Corpo Santo, and co-labourers in the city of Cork. Rivals only in the cause of religion, they were closely united by ties of the deepest affection. Like his friend, John Pius Leahy was a

[61] This monument was designed by Mr. Hynes, and executed by Mr. O'Connell, sculptor, with the exception of the bust, which was the work of Thomas O'Farrell, R.H.A., Dublin.

VERY REV. B. T. RUSSELL, O.P.

native of Cork. Born on the 25th July, 1802, he went when fifteen years old to Corpo Santo. Having made his profession in the Dominican Order, he was ordained in 1825, and was immediately assigned to teach various branches of ecclesiastical subjects—philosophy, theology, and the history of the Church—being thus employed for fifteen years. He was likewise rector of the college of Corpo Santo, founded by the celebrated Dominic O'Daly, a native of Kerry.[62] Father Leahy was elected prior of the Dominican Convent of Cork in 1847, and was subsequently Provincial of Ireland. In this capacity he attended the Synod of Thurles in 1850. Deservedly held in high repute as a theologian, he was appointed Master of Conference for the diocese of Cork.

Such was the career of this great man before he was compelled, in 1854, to leave the retirement so dear to him, in order to become coadjutor-bishop to Dr. Blake in the diocese of Dromore. The latter dying six years subsequently, Dr. Leahy succeeded to him, and governed the diocese for thirty years. He ruled his flock mildly but firmly, spreading everywhere the sweet odour of his virtues, being specially remarkable for profound humility, which pervaded his every movement. Though gifted above most men with the power of eloquence—by reason of which he was considered the first pulpit orator in Ireland—he shrank instinctively from the public gaze, and loved nothing better than retirement. Nevertheless, was he

[62] Also called " Dominic of the Rosary."

ever ready to make church or oratory resound with words of light and charm, when prompted by the call of duty or charity.

MOST REV. DR. LEAHY, O.P.
(*Late Bishop of Dromore.*)

During his episcopate Dr. Leahy had always at heart the advancement of religion, and under his paternal care the Poor Clares and Sisters of Mercy were introduced into Newry, as well as the latter into

Rostrevor and Lurgan. In Newry also during his time were established the Dominican Church and Priory of St. Catherine. Many other churches and schools, besides religious bodies, owe their existence in Dromore to its honoured bishop, who until his death was ever the same unassuming Father Leahy that was loved and revered by the people of Cork.

If humility be the foundation of all other virtues, there is little doubt that Dr. Leahy had reached the climax to which this virtue leads, true nobility and sanctity of soul, combined with a holiness of life to which few can attain. No wonder then that his death, like his life, was considered that of a saint. His obsequies were celebrated in the cathedral of Newry on the 9th September, 1890, and were attended by an immense concourse of people, besides many prelates, amongst whom was Dr. O'Callaghan, O.P., celebrant on the occasion. The remains of the deceased bishop were laid in the cemetery attached to the "old chapel" of Newry, where for some years the Dominicans had officiated.

The Most Rev. Joseph Larocca, general of the Order, died in January, 1891. His successor, Father Frühwirth, a native of Austria, was elected at Oulins, near Lyons, on the 20th of September. Being a man of great learning, he was appointed master of studies in the Dominican Convent of Gratz in 1876, and more than once declined the episcopal dignity.[63]

[63] Only on three occasions in six hundred years has an Austrian been elected General of the Dominican Order.

About this time two altars of exquisite design and superior workmanship were erected in the Church, Pope's Quay.[64] We are indebted for these altars to Miss Susan Murphy, who bequeathed one thousand pounds to the community of St. Mary's. She was sister of the late Count Murphy, and Nicholas Murphy of Carrigmore.

The writer avails of this opportunity to express his own and his brethren's heartfelt gratitude to this well-known and distinguished family, and to give them the earnest assurance of constant remembrance in the prayers of the community.

Amongst the many deceased friends of the Cork Dominicans was one who was connected with them from his boyhood, and whose memory shall be ever held in the most affectionate esteem. Mr. Thomas Bresnan was a man of rare virtue, and conspicuous for uprightness of character and holiness of life. A faithful member of the Society of St. Vincent de Paul, and attached from his youth to the Sodality of the Holy Name (established at St. Mary's for the teaching of catechism on Sundays), he scrupulously observed the rules of these societies, and was united with both up to his death. The members of the Sodality,

---

[64] The plans were drawn by Mr. Hynes, and the work executed by Messrs. Daly and Son, Cook Street. The group surmounting the altar of our Lady, and the statue over that of St. Dominic, were wrought and erected by Mr. Smyth, of Dublin—the former at the expense of the female branch of the Confraternity of the Rosary, and the latter at the expense of the Sodality of St. Thomas Aquinas.

appreciating his high qualities, elected him president each succeeding year.

At the inauguration of the Young Men's Society at St. Mary's, by the late Dr. Leahy, Mr. Bresnan was amongst those present. He was subsequently appointed vice-president, which position he filled with honour for twenty-five years, when on the retirement of the president, Mr. John George McCarthy, he was elected his successor. Resigning after two years, he was presented by the members with his portrait, accompanied by an address and testimonial. Some years before his death—having resigned the presidentship of the Sodality of the Holy Name—his fellow-labourers likewise gave him a beautifully illuminated address. It was as follows :—

"ADDRESS OF THE SODALITY OF THE HOLY NAME OF ST. MARY'S CORK,
To the President, THOMAS BRESNAN, Esq., on his resignation of his Office, March, 1889.

VERY DEAR PRESIDENT,

We cannot allow your half-century of edifying labours in the service of our Sodality to close without addressing to you our sincere gratitude for the many tokens of good will and kindness in all your relations with us, as well as the sense of our loss at your resignation of the Presidential Office, so long illustrated by your virtue, which, like the lamp before the shrine, ever showed us light to guide us on our way, and as a gentle zephyr fanned into flame the flagging zeal of our members.

It is now fifty years since you joined our Sodality, at a time when the struggle of our faith had still to be fought—when true and sturdy hearts and willing hands were still needed to build our Churches and our Convents—when the heavy chain of intolerance, though freshly unbound from our limbs, had still left its canker-wounds and its dismal marks on our manhood; St. Mary's had indeed emerged from the obscurity of Friary Lane, and its muffled bell had been replaced by the melodious Angelus-peal, but the members of the Order were yet housed in the Old Friary of Dominick Street. In the meantime religious bigotry held high sway in our city, though the long night of serfdom was fast passing away before the rising sun of Catholic freedom. And foremost in the van of that mighty change, you were ever ready in the ranks of the zealous, self-sacrificing band, whose work (accomplished in one generation) we see in Catholic Cork of to-day—studded as it is, with glorious temples, and still more glorious institutions.

Besides your multifarious and noble labours in other spheres of action, nearest of all we think of your life-long connection with the Dominican Order, and the Sodality of the Holy Name. We shall always associate your never-failing presence, and silent, but most persuasive example, with the exalted objects aimed at by our Sodality, and with the pious practice of its rules.

We too, with you, have often heard the good counsels of the venerated patriarch Dr. Russell, the founder of the St. Mary's branch of the Sodality of the Holy Name; of the Most Rev. Dr. Leahy, bishop of Dromore, holiest and wisest of men; of Dr. Carbery, the chosen friend and apostle of youth; of the gentle ascetic Father Conway, truest of friends; and of the long line of saintly sons of St. Dominic (including our own venerated Bishop), who have dwelt and laboured in St. Mary's Cork—their memory will be ever green in our hearts, while their wise words, let us hope, have not been quite unfruitful in shaping our actions and our lives.

In conclusion, while we deeply regret that your resignation of office is unavoidable, we trust and pray that God will spare you many years of restored health, still to edify us, and still to be—

'Like the oak by the fountain in sunshine and storm,
Like the rock on the mountain unchanging in form,

Like the course of our river through ages the same,
Like the dew rising ever to heaven, whence it came.

Signed on behalf of the Sodality,

JAMES A. DWYER, O.P., *Spiritual Director.*
PATRICK HEGARTY, *Vice-President.*
JAMES A. SULLIVAN, *Secretary.*"

It is only right to add that this eloquent address, which was illuminated with exquisite taste and in the most perfect style by Mr. Brennan, a young local artist, was composed by Laurence O'Sullivan, Esq., afterwards and still the revered vice-president of the Sodality.

Mr. Bresnan died at his residence, Patrick's Hill, on the 1st May, 1893. R. I. P.

A circular letter was received by the Prior of St. Mary's on the 16th September of this year, relative to the death and glorious career of Cardinal Zigliara, O.P., who died in Rome on the 10th May previous. Having been elevated to the purple, he was appointed by Leo XIII. prefect of a committee of Dominican fathers, to whom was entrusted the revision of the works of St. Thomas, and before his death had the pleasure of seeing published many volumes of the new edition, which by desire of his Holiness is now entirely under the control of the Dominican General.[65]

In 1894 the community of St. Mary's lost one of their young priests, the Rev. A. M. McGowan, who

---

[65] One member of this committee (Very Rev. James Littleton) is an Irishman.

died in the prime of life, being only twenty-eight years old. He had laboured in the city somewhat more than three years, and was remarkable for wonderful zeal both in pulpit and confessional. At his death, which took place on the 20th March, he left many sincere friends to mourn his loss.

He was born in Carlingford, county Louth, under the shadow of the ruins of an ancient Dominican convent, which very probably was the means of directing the course of his after life. With reason do we apply to him the words of Holy Writ : " Being made perfect in a short space, he fulfilled a long time." *Wisdom*, chap. iv. His remains lie in the cemetery attached to the church.

Within the lapse of four months the Rev. Gabriel Moore, O.P., was called to his reward.[66] He was a young priest of great promise, being highly cultivated, and conspicuous for sterling virtue and goodness of heart. Having completed his studies at San Clemente, Rome, he was about leaving for Ireland, when suddenly taken ill he departed this life on the 25th July, 1894, not having been yet three years ordained.

The Bishop of Cloyne, Most Rev. Dr. Browne, visited Youghal a short time after his consecration, and received addresses from various bodies in the town. Amongst them was one from the Presentation Convent Schools. In his answer, the Bishop alluded to the Franciscan and Dominican houses which had

---

[66] **He was brother of Father Moore, then Prior of St. Mary's.**

formerly existed in Youghal, and in reference to the latter expressed himself thus :—" There was another monastery in this great old town—a Dominican monastery—also amongst the earliest foundations of the great Dominican Order in Ireland, and in that monastery was a famous statue of 'Our Lady of Graces.' May I not conclude that it is that Mother of Graciousness who has watched over this great old Catholic town, and that it is owing to her intercession with our Divine Lord that the faith has been preserved through every phase of difficulty and trial, so that now it has come to our lot to see once again in this town a display of Catholicity, such as must give comfort to the heart of a bishop."

The consecration of the new side altars in the church, Pope's Quay, took place on the 5th February, 1895, during the celebration of a solemn Triduum, which opened the previous Sunday. The altar of St. Dominic was consecrated by Dr. Browne, whilst the Bishop of Cork performed a like ceremony at that of the Rosary, over which was placed the miraculous statue of "Our Lady of Graces." An overflowing congregation attended each evening of the Triduum, and eloquent sermons were preached by the Venerable Archdeacon Coughlan, Blackrock ; Rev. Lewis Butler, O.P., of Dublin, and Very Rev. Canon Keller, P.P., Youghal. On the third day high mass was celebrated in presence of his Lordship Dr. O'Callaghan by the Very Rev. Father Moore, O.P.

Presuming that a somewhat detailed description of

this memorable celebration would interest our readers, I have added the following account:—

THE CELEBRATION OF A SOLEMN TRIDUUM IN THE CHURCH OF ST. MARY'S, CORK.

On the evening of Sunday, February 3rd, 1895, a Solemn Triduum was opened in the Dominican Church. It had a triple object—the formal inauguration of the new side altars and the marble statues surmounting them, the consecration of the altars, and the installation of the image of " Our Lady of Graces" above the altar of the Rosary.

The Most Rev. Dr. O'Callaghan, O.P., presided, and the devotions commenced with procession of the Rosary, in which the prior and community, with his lordship the bishop, the Venerable Archdeacon Coghlan, and also the members of the confraternities of the Rosary, the Holy Name, and St. Thomas of Aquin, took part. An overflowing congregation attended, as also on the other days of the triduum. Archdeacon Coghlan, P.P., Blackrock, then delivered a beautiful and impressive discourse on devotion to the Blessed Virgin, taking for his text the words of the " Magnificat," " Behold from henceforth all nations shall call me blessed." Having enlarged in eloquent terms on the virtues and prerogatives of Mary, and having alluded to the procession which had just taken place, as a small recognition on the part of those present in her honour, the venerable preacher concluded by saying "that on such an evening, and in such a church, it would be unpardonable in him to omit referring to one whom he might, in a most emphatic manner, style the apostle of devotion to Mary. If ever there was a saint in the history of the church whose zeal and reverence and whose enthusiasm and personal worth entitled him to be called the privileged apostle of devotion to Mary, it was St. Dominic. That evening they were to have unveiled before them a beautiful marble group representing Our Blessed Lady giving the Rosary to St. Dominic." The preacher then described the devotion of the Rosary, and thus concluded his discourse. Immediately afterwards the group of statues was blessed by the Bishop. The statue of St. Dominic surmounting his own altar was blessed on a previous occasion.

The side altars of Our Blessed Lady and St. Dominic were consecrated on Monday, at ten o'clock, the former by the bishop of the diocese, and the latter by the Most Rev. Dr. Browne, the bishop of Cloyne. They are of elaborate construction, and were designed by Mr. Hynes, architect, and executed by Mr. Daly, builder, in the most exquisite and artistic manner, the style being Corinthian, in keeping with that of the church. A curved coning in the superstructure of each altar forms a niche, lit from behind, in which respectively is the group of statues and the statue of St. Dominic, which have been alluded to already. A tabernacle of beautifully-wrought brass on the Rosary altar is surmounted by a marble structure which now contains the image of Our Lady of Youghal.

On Monday evening the devotions of the triduum were resumed, and consisted, as on the previous evening, of procession of the Rosary, sermon, and benediction of the most Holy Sacrament. The sermon was preached by the Rev. Lewis Butler, o.p., of St. Saviour's, Dublin, and was listened to with rapt attention by the congregation. He said that many instances were recorded in sacred scripture of how, in moments of supreme national peril and impending ruin, the people of God were rescued by the hand of a woman. He made special mention in this respect of Deborah, Judith, and the mother of the Machabees, but remarked that they were only the figures and precursors of one greater than them all, and that was the humble Virgin of Nazareth, the mother of Jesus Christ. Mary, by her agency, saved not one generation but all the generations of men. Referring to St. Dominic, Father Butler said that when struggling with the Albigensian heresy he preached in vain, until one night the Blessed Virgin appeared and presented to him the holy Rosary. Whilst afterwards employing this spiritual weapon the most hardened sinners were softened by his words, and thousands of heretics were saved by the power and prayers of a woman. He then spoke of Ireland, and said that persecution had done its utmost to destroy the faith of our country. The broken arches, the burned shrines, the ivy-clad walls, the land thrice confiscated, told all that she had suffered in the cause of truth and justice. But there was one thing left, and this could never be snatched from the bleeding hands of Ireland. That was the Catholic faith. The reason of this unchangeable fidelity was to be found in our devotion to the holy mother of God—a devotion handed down from father to son and mother to daughter, until it became an heirloom in every Irish Catholic household.

Tuesday was the closing day of the triduum. High mass was celebrated at eleven o'clock by the prior (Father Moore) in the presence of the bishop. He also presided at the evening devotions, which began with procession in honour of "Our Lady of Graces." The Very Rev. Canon Keller, P.P., of Youghal, preached. The Fathers of St. Mary's considered it not only most becoming but also a great privilege that Canon Keller should preach at the close of this solemn triduum, as it was principally intended to honour "Our Lady of Graces," whose sacred image formerly belonged to his parish, and he himself was so distinguished an ecclesiastic, being revered as such both by his brethern of the priesthood and the entire Catholic laity of Ireland. The priests of Cloyne, when about to choose one of their body to be their bishop, placed his name as *dignissimus* at the head of the list of those deemed worthy for the exalted position. And to the laity he appeared, even to those who differed with him in his political action, as the "good shepherd" or pastor, being prepared to suffer imprisonment, as he did, and even what was worse, suspicion and coldness on the part of his superiors, rather than betray the flock entrusted to his care, or their interests when at stake.

In his sermon, Canon Keller delicately and beautifully connected the marvellous merits of "Our Lady of the Rosary" with those of "Our Lady of Graces," for whilst dilating on the former he brought the minds of his hearers to dwell on the latter. "That occasion," he said, "was specially dear to him, when, for the first time after the lapse of many generations, the venerable figure of 'Our Lady of Youghal' was exposed for public veneration and devotion; and being an occasion too that had been blessed in a special manner by our most holy father the Pope, under the patronage of the venerated prelate of this diocese." Having spoken of the great devotion and confidence in Mary which prevailed in this truly Catholic land, he said that "he did not know a nation in all the pages of the history of the church where the Catholic faith had been more steadfastly adhered to, or where greater sufferings or sacrifices were made for the faith than in Ireland. Meanwhile churches were levelled to the earth, shrines were burnt and altars overthrown, but the figure of 'Our Lady of Youghal' was saved; and he envied them, while he congratulated them, on possessing that sacred relic, which for a long succession of ages, in the old time of Youghal by the sea, was a source of veneration and attraction to countless multitudes of our forefathers."

At the conclusion of the sermon, benediction of the most Holy Sacrament was given by his lordship the Bishop, and thus terminated this memorable triduum, which abounded with so many tokens of deep piety and love on the part of the Catholics of Cork towards the mother of God in her hope-inspiring character of "Our Lady of Graces."

A PUBLIC APPEAL FOR FUNDS TO REPAIR AND IMPROVE
ST. MARY'S CHURCH, POPE'S QUAY.

In a leading article of one [67] of the local papers the remarks transferred to these pages appeared in its issue of the 24th of February, 1896. They refer to an appeal which was made on the previous day by the community of St. Mary's to the citizens of Cork, for funds to enable the Fathers to make certain necessary repairs and improvements in their church.

[67] The *Daily Herald*.

" Catholic Cork has reason to be proud of the result of yesterday's meeting in St. Mary's Church. Convened for the purpose of raising funds for the preservation and improvement of the beautiful structure in charge of the Dominican Fathers, the meeting was thoroughly representative of the leading citizens, and successful beyond the most sanguine expectations of the promoters . . . . In a city famed for its liberality on behalf of every movement appealing to the charitable and religious instincts of its people, another proof has been given . . . . of the boundless generosity of which it is capable, when a worthy object, such as that of yesterday's meeting, is concerned . . . . St. Mary's Church is one of the many sacred edifices of which Cork can justly boast. It is also in charge of an Order which has played a memorable part in the extension of the Catholic faith in all parts of the world, and in its preservation in Ireland when penal laws were enacted to extinguish it . . . . Since their establishment amongst us in Cork, the Dominican Fathers have worked indefatigably in the sacred cause of religion. The Church of St. Mary's has been the scene of their unselfish labour for nearly sixty years. It is a structure of much architectural beauty, and is frequented by a large congregation. But the effects of time have told on its condition, and the work of restoring and preserving it in a fit state cannot be longer delayed . . . . We need only refer our readers to the statement made by the Rev. Prior (Father Moore) to convince them of the urgency of the appeal. The citizens who attended the meeting did their part in a manner worthy of their Irish faith."

Important Public Meeting.

The Catholics of Cork assembled in great numbers in St. Mary's Church, on Sunday, February 23rd, 1896, for the purpose of raising funds to defray the expenses already incurred, or to be incurred, by the community in making necessary repairs and improvements in the church.

The Prior, Very Rev. Father Moore, proposed that Mr. Nicholas

Murphy (Carrigmore) would take the chair, and the motion was received with acclamation by all present.

Amongst those were—Rev. Father O'Sullivan, o.s.a.; Rev. Father McSwiney, o.s.a.; Rev. Father O'Mahony, o.s.a.; Alderman P. J. Madden, Messrs. P. J. Hegarty, John McDonnell, James Murphy, M. D. Daly, j.p.; Edward Ryan, Lieut.-Colonel Murray, M. P. Buckley, j.p.; Peter O'Flynn, Thomas Crosbie, A. M. Cole, t.c.; Maurice O'Donnell, t.c.; M. C. Daly, t.c.; Francis Curtin, Dominick O'Leary, D. J. Twomey, P. Fielding, P. Tracey, P. Kirwan, John Canty, P. Cahill, John English, James Hogan, Christopher J. Dunn, j.p.; L. O'Sullivan, Joseph Deyos, Thomas Attridge, J. McCormick, J. J. Nunan, G. Moran, J. A. Hanrahan, S. F. Hynes, John Twomey, P. Moriarty, J. Cahill, F. J. Murphy, Pierce Roche, John G. McCarthy, C. O'Sullivan, James J. Scanlan, Michael McCarthy, t.c.; D. J. O'Mahony, John O'Connor, William Ryan, M. J. Barry, h.c.; Thomas Travers, John Riordan, W. Smiddy, T. J. Cagney, E. McNamara, P. J. Riordan, T. J. Sheedy, D. J. Lucy, t.c.; D. Fitzpatrick, J. H. Sugrue, John Ryan, John Cross, N. Cole, J. Nolan, John Murphy, Thomas Mullins, A. Henley, Stephen Perry, j.p.; Ignatius Harrington, Edward Geary, P. Barrett, Jerome Twomey, R. Tivy, B. M. Egan, Timothy Kiely, James O'Reilly, John Perry, R. J. Murphy, hon. sec. Cork Young Men's Society; W. J. Cahill, T. J. Clanchy, h.c.; Dr. Brown, Michael McCarthy, C. O'Connell, Thomas Mockler, John Galgey, C. Paul, R. O'Hanlon. The following members of the community were also present—Rev. Father Moore, Rev. Father Dwyer, Rev. Father Masterson, Rev. Father Walsh, Rev. Father O'Kane, Rev. Father Quinn, Rev. Father Howard, and Rev. Father Duggan.

The following report was read by Father Moore. I will lay before you, gentlemen, what we have done and what we intend to do. From time to time portions of the overhanging acanthus leaves of the capitals of the pillars, through damp or other causes, became detached and fell to the ground, but fortunately at times when the church was empty. Early last year a considerable portion of one of the capitals fell, and this caused us serious anxiety as to the condition of the ceiling. On examination, however, we found it to be, on the whole, in a perfectly sound state; the wood-work behind was in excellent order, and the stucco adhered to the wood, and was firmly knit together. Still, to reassure those frequenting the church, we asked the architect, Mr. Hynes, to report fully on the matter, and to offer such suggestions as he deemed advisable. He accordingly laid before the community three plans: (1) To remove the ceiling altogether, and to substitute one in wood or light fibrous plaster; (2) to remove the stucco capitals of the pillars, and the heavier ornaments of the entablature and panels, and to replace them with others of wood; (3) to secure all the ornaments with strong copper wire, to strengthen the deeply undercut leaves, and to saturate the entire surface of the stucco with an indurating material, which would render it proof against damp caused by the condensation of hot air. Acting under the advice of the architect, we determined to adopt the third plan. Thus we shall provide for the safety of those who frequent the church, without spoiling the classic ceiling and its ornaments. As the indurating material referred to is supplied in various tints, we applied a few subdued tones of colour in order to bring out into stronger relief the different sections of architraves, frieze, medallions, etc. Provision is being made, moreover, for the more effectual ventilation of the church by adding glass hoppers to the windows, and opening near the ceiling of the aisles several chimney shafts, originally made in the main walls for purposes long since abandoned. Other works which we intend to carry through without further delay are the decoration of the apse and the reconstruction of the organ, retaining some of the stops and incorporating them in the new instrument, or the erection of an entirely new organ. A most important work, likewise, is the renewal of the leaden gutters of the roof and side towers. The present gutters have been repaired again and again, and it is with difficulty that we can keep the water out. Nearly thirty years have elapsed since we made an appeal to our friends, but at length urgent necessity compels us to solicit their help, as we have no resources of our own, and we feel assured that their response will be in keeping with the more than friendly interest they have ever shown in this church and community.

The Chairman said he was sure the citizens of Cork would not turn a deaf ear to the appeal which Father Moore had made. On the contrary, they would give promptly and liberally on this occasion. He then called on Mr. Crosbie to propose the first resolution.

Mr. Crosbie said the task of proposing the first resolution had been very much simplified by the statement they had heard from the Father Prior of that church and community. He believed that that church had been in existence for about sixty years, and his own memory assured him of the fact. That church had always been an object of pride and admiration to the citizens of Cork. But the church had more than its external beauty to recommend it. It had entwined in its history associations which were dear to them. There were names in connection with it that still awake a thrill of pride and gratitude in the hearts of Corkmen. Many still amongst them remembered the saintly Bishop of Dromore; few of the seniors had forgotten Bishop Carbery, and surely the memory of Dr. Russell was still green in the hearts of many of their fellow-townsmen. These great men had found successors worthy of them, who had kept alive the traditions and the teaching and the splendid example they afforded to those who surrounded them, and they now asked the citizens of Cork to aid them in maintaining the noble temple in which they all worshipped. The fathers whom they saw around them in their white robes would pass away as their predecessors had passed away, and, like them, he had no doubt would be held in honour and gratitude amongst the community, but the church would remain. The servants of the temple depart, but the temple remains. The edifice was one of which the citizens of Cork would be always proud, and when the Dominicans asked them to help in preserving it, they were simply asking the worshippers to work for themselves. Having said so much, he would conclude by moving this simple and straightforward resolution—"That the works undertaken by the Dominican Fathers, for the preservation and improvement of their beautiful church, are absolutely necessary."

Mr. C. J. Dunn seconded the resolution, and observed that after the lucid explanation of the works which they heard detailed by Father Moore, and the admirable manner in which Mr. Crosbie had developed the question, very little remained to be said. The external works were such as were absolutely necessary in a climate of this kind that suffered particularly from rain-fall and humidity of every kind, and they had heard it was absolutely necessary to secure the roof in order to keep out the rain. The community did not incur any unnecessary expense in undertaking these works; they were only doing what was absolutely necessary. He believed they would agree with him that the community adopted the right course in approving of the improvements suggested by the architect, by which the edifice would lose none of its internal beauty. He was quite sure the citizens would appreciate in a practical manner that the works undertaken were of a thoroughly necessary character.

The resolution was passed unanimously.

Mr. A. M. Cole proposed the next resolution as follows :— "That considering the Dominican Fathers have not appealed to the generosity of their fellow-citizens for the last thirty years, and having no resources of their own, it is the opinion of this meeting that their appeal is worthy of the warmest support of the public." Mr. Crosbie, he said, had so fully compassed the ground that very little remained for him to say in support of the resolution entrusted to his care. He was certain the citizens of Cork would open their hearts and purses to this appeal, and remove any anxiety from the minds of the Fathers to whom this church had been entrusted, and that their appeal would meet with a ready, willing, and liberal response.

Mr. James Scanlan, in seconding the resolution, said his earliest recollections were associated with that church. That magnificent meeting was a guarantee that the Dominican Fathers would get what they required, and that the church would be preserved in its beauty and elegance, and would remain so when the Fathers had passed away.

THE DOMINICANS.

Alderman Madden proposed "That a subscription list be now opened." He looked upon that resolution as being pre-eminently the resolution of the day. He was sure that the appeal made by the good Fathers of St. Mary's would be met in a generous spirit; and if it was not, he was mistaken in the people of Cork. He did not think that there was a community that leant less on the people of that city in his time than the Dominican Fathers. It was now thirty years since they made an appeal to the people of Cork, and it was a marvel to him how they sustained that edifice for such a length of time out of their own resources.

Mr. John Rearden seconded the resolution, which was carried unanimously.

On the motion of Father Moore, Messrs. Frank Murphy and Ignatius Harrington were appointed treasurers to the fund; and Messrs. Stephen Perry, James O'Sullivan, Richard Twomey, and John Galgey, secretaries. He announced that a number of subscriptions were already sent in.

A collection was then made, and a very large number of subscriptions were handed in.

Father Moore, on behalf of the community, returned thanks to Mr. Nicholas Murphy for presiding. He had been always, he said, to them a true and good friend, and they did not know how to thank him sufficiently for his kindness on that and every other occasion. He had also to thank the gentlemen who had spoken to the resolutions, and all their generous benefactors.

The proceedings then terminated.

The entire amount realized by this appeal exceeded £1,600. This generosity was but a sequel to the numberless proofs, which the citizens of Cork had given through a long succession of years, of their unalterable attachment to the Dominicans, who for so many centuries have laboured without interruption in the city by the Lee.

SECOND PART—COUNTY.

Youghal and the Miraculous Statue.

"It is one long chaplet of memories,
 Tender and true and sweet,
That gleam in the past and the distance,
 Like lamps that burn at her feet.

Like stars that will shine for ever,
 For time cannot touch or stir
The graces that Mary has given,
 Or the trust that we give to her."

ADELAIDE A. PROCTER.

THE Dominican Convent of Youghal,[68] county Cork, was founded in 1268 by Thomas, son of Maurice Fitzgerald, then Viceroy of Ireland, under the title of "Lord Justiciary." In 1243, John, his paternal grandfather, founded the priory in Tralee, where he was buried. The remains of Thomas were laid in the cemetery of the Youghal Convent, which was dedicated to the Holy Cross, probably on account of the red cross marked on his family shield.[69] The

---

[68] A view of the town, including this convent, appears in Smith's *History of Cork*, vol. i., book ii., chap. i.

[69] *Hib. Dom.*, pp. 239, 272-73. This title was changed in course of time to "Our Lady of Graces," as will be seen in the account of the miraculous statue.

houses of Tralee and Sligo, built by the Geraldines, as well as five others of the Order in Ireland, and that of Louvain, bore the same appellation.

The Friary of Youghal was built to the north of the town,[70] and though the dwelling has totally disappeared, the ruins of the church may still be seen surrounded by monuments of the dead. Judging from the foundations, which have occasionally been uncovered, it consisted of nave, choir, and south aisle.[71] The dwelling was situated, according to conventional custom, on the north side. There still exists to south-east a massive though mutilated pier, which supported the arches as well as the west end of the nave, and fragments of the side walls. There can be little doubt but that it was a beautiful church, and no mean specimen of the Gothic style in the thirteenth century, as can be seen by the foliated capitals still adhering to the pier.

Above the west doorway was a three-light window, which all but fills the entire gable. Tradition tells us that a subterranean passage, running in a southerly direction, connected the Priory with St. Mary's Collegiate Church. When in 1847 a grave was being dug in the cemetery for the body of a man named

---

[70] To the south was the Franciscan Convent, founded in 1260 by Gerald Fitzgerald, brother of Thomas (Ware, *de Antiquitatibus Hib.*, chap. 26, p. 146). Others assert that William de Vesey was the founder. The beautiful Presentation Nunnery now occupies the site.

[71] The measurements, exclusive of walls, were—Nave, 73 feet by 24 feet 8 inches; choir, 66 feet by 24 feet 8 inches; and south aisle, 105 feet by 21 feet.—Rev. Samuel Hayman, A.B.

CONVENT OF YOUGHAL.

Broderick, there was found a freestone effigy of a knight in armour, with a sword at his side. The coffin was placed over the effigy, which is still supposed to be undisturbed.[72] The convent lands were given by the English Government to various persons successively—first, in 1581, to a military man named William Walsh, at a nominal rent of twenty-two pence for ever; then for a term of years to John Thickpenny, who was also a soldier. As certified in the "MS. of Lismore," by A. St. Leger, the Friary was granted to Walter Raleigh on the 3rd of February, 1586, at an annual rent of £12 19s. 6d.[73] All his Irish grants were conveyed by Raleigh to Mr. Richard Boyle, the first Lord Cork, on the 7th December, 1602.[74] The buildings were, however, destroyed in the following year, and the agents whom Raleigh employed for the purpose were, according to authentic accounts, most unfortunate. The first who undertook the demolition fell dead from the roof of the church, all his limbs being broken; also three soldiers, who threw the Holy Cross from the top of the monastry, met with frightful deaths. Within eight days of the outrage one died insane, another was consumed by vermin, and the third killed by the seneschal of the Earl of Desmond.[75]

[72] Article by Rev. S. Hayman, A.B., *Kilkenny Archæological Journal*, 1854-55, p. 333.
[73] A proviso was made in the deed that the Act passed in Limerick, anno. 33 of Henry VIII., for lands given by the king, should not be prejudicial to this deed.
[74] Patent Rolls.
[75] *Theatre of Catholique and Protestant Religion*, p. 124.

The following were distinguished members of the Youghal community :—Dominic O'Ronain, who having completed his studies at Louvain, was appointed master of novices in 1654. This position he held for ten years, and then returned to Youghal,

FRIARY OF YOUGHAL.

where he zealously fulfilled his priestly duties for a considerable time. Raymond O'Fahadh, who had made his studies at Victoria, in Spain, and was an eloquent preacher. James O'Henny, who also studied in Spain. His excellent qualities were the subject of praise on the part of O'Heyne, O.P., in his *Epilogus Chronologicus*.

quoted by the Rev. S. Hayman in his *Book on Youghal*; also, *Hib. Dom.*, p. 273.

The Miraculous Statue.

"HOLY CROSS," the title of the convent of Youghal, was changed to that of "Our Lady of Graces," because of a statue of the Blessed Virgin, which the Friars obtained in a miraculous manner. A piece of wood brought in by the tide was found on the river's bank adjoining the town. This wood being rare in the locality some fishermen wished to appropriate it, but they were unable to lift it though they harnessed ten horses for the purpose. The ebbing tide bearing it towards the Dominican Convent, two of the religious brought it to the cloister. The Prior being informed in a vision, which he had during the night, that the image of Our Lady, the "Virgin of Great Power," was in this wood, found it accordingly.[76]

Another account tells us that the piece of timber was exposed to the weather near the porch of the church. A blind man entering the building, and seeking with outstretched hand for holy water, dipped his fingers into the rain water lodged in a cavity of the

---

[76] *Les Voyages et Observations du Sieur Boullaye le Gouz*, p. 454, published 1653. This author was called by his contemporaries the "Catholic Traveller," having visited all the countries of the world.

STATUE AND OLD AND NEW SHRINE OF OUR LADY OF YOUGHAL.

wood. Thinking it was holy water he at once washed his eyes, according to his custom, and on the instant his sight was restored. This miracle led to the examination of the wood and the consequent discovery of the image. This image was the object of special devotion to the faithful, who flocked from all parts of Ireland to venerate it.

By a decree of the Most General Chapter,[77] held in Rome, 1644, all alms offered in honour of the pious image were to be applied to the convent of Youghal, and the Provincial was ordered not to dispose of them otherwise.

This statue of the Madonna and Child is of Italian workmanship of the fifteenth century. It is a carving in ivory about three inches long, much worn and discoloured by time.[78]

During the persecutions the Dominicans removed the image to a place of safety. It was afterwards enclosed by a daughter of one of the Geraldines in a silver case, richly decorated with floriated ornaments and surmounted by a cross. In front are folding doors, which when open display the sacred relic. On the inside of the doors are a crucifixion and the figure of a saint respectively. The case bears the following

---

[77] The ordinations of a Most General Chapter are equal in force to those of three ordinary General Chapters, and bind in perpetuity.—*Hib. Dom.*, p. 114.

[78] To the pencil of Mrs. Collins, the daughter of the late James Roche, the "Roscoe" of Cork, is to be attributed the front view of the shrine, which with the image is beautifully illustrated in the *Ulster Journal of Archæology*, April, 1854.

Latin inscription:—*Orate pro anima Onoriæ filiæ Jacobi de Geraldinis quæ me fieri fecit. Anno Domini*, 1617. "Pray for the soul of Honoria, daughter of James Fitzgerald, who caused me to be made. A.D. 1617."

It will be interesting to add here a letter of Crofton Croker to the Rev. James J. Carbery, O.P., afterwards the bishop of Hamilton, in Canada.

"3 Gloucester Road,
Old Brompton, London,
24*th October*, 1853.

REV. AND DEAR SIR,

I beg to thank you most sincerely for your kindness in forwarding to me the very beautiful drawings I have received with your letter of the 21st instant, and I hope when you next communicate with Dr. Russell you will do me the favour to convey to him my acknowledgments, which I have now the pleasure to express to you.

The shrine was for a few days in my custody, through the kindness of my lamented friend, the late Mr. James Roche, who assisted me in my translation of M. Boullaye de Gouz's tour in Ireland in 1644, by whom it is supposed to be mentioned. We differed, I think, about the identity of the lady who presented the shrine to the Dominicans, Mr. Roche conjecturing hastily, as I still think, that she was a Countess of Desmond, whereas I believed Honoria (Onoriæ) to be the daughter of Sir James Desmond who was killed in 1597 by the sons of Sir William Bourke, and whose body was gibbetted at Kilmallock. This lady was married to her relative, John Fitzgerald, seneschal of Imokilly, and after his death to Sir Edmond, son and heir of Sir John Fitzgerald, of Cloyne and Ballymaloe.

It is altogether a most interesting relic, and allow me to add to my expression 'beautiful drawings'—a far higher comment from an antiquarian—'and most accurate.'

If at any time I can be of service to you in this neighbourhood, believe it will give me sincere pleasure, and that I remain very truly,
>
> Your obedient and humble servant,
> T. CROFTON CROKER.

The Rev. James J. Carbery,
    etc., etc."

It is well to remark that Honoria Fitzgerald was not the long-lived Countess of Desmond who was called Catherine, and whose father was Sir John of Dromana, nor was she daughter of Sir James Desmond, slain by Bourke in 1597, but of James, fifteenth Earl of Desmond, long known as "the pretended Earl."[79]

During a temporary cessation of the persecutions the Dominicans returned to Youghal, but were compelled to leave owing to the Act passed on the 1st May, 1698, commanding all religious orders to depart from Ireland. They then entrusted the sacred image to Sir John Hore, of Shandon Castle, county Waterford;[80] but we find it again in the hands of the Dominicans once more residing in Youghal in 1756. The community consisted of three priests, Thomas O'Kelly, prior, Dominic Houghlahan, and James Flynn.

From the time of its discovery up to our own days miraculous powers have been uninterruptedly ascribed to the image of "Our Lady of Graces," and as long as

---

[79] *Religious Foundations of Youghal* by Rev. Samuel Hayman, and *History of Cork* by Rev. C. B. Gibson.
[80] *Hib. Dom.*, p. 273.

it was possible the Irish people made pilgrimages to the Friary of Youghal in order to honour it.[81]

Amongst the frequent instances of cures and graces obtained by prayers offered in honour of this image was that of Mr. Michael O'Callaghan, father of the present bishop of Cork. The new shrine is a votive offering of thanksgiving for his recovery, and bears the following inscription:—*Sanctæ Mariæ Gratiarum Michael O'Callaghan Familiaque devote Gratias agentes, A.D. MDCCCLXXII.* "Michael O'Callaghan and family devoutly returning thanks to Saint Mary of Graces, 1872." This shrine was designed by the late Mr. Goldie, of London. The work was executed in Paris, under his personal supervision. Mr. Goldie would accept no remuneration for his own eminent personal services, as he was desirous of participating in the noble offering of the donors.

This venerable image is now in the possession of the Dominican community of Cork. No precise record exists as to the manner in which it came into their hands, but the following may throw light upon the subject. In the dark days of persecution it was ordained by the authorities of the Order in Ireland that when, as frequently happened, the inmates of a

---

[81] The following appears in the Register of the Order of St. Dominic:—"In the year 1639, 19th February, Father James Hurley was confirmed Provincial of Ireland, having been elected in the Chapter assembled on the 12th October, in the convent of 'Our Lady of Graces' of Youghal." He was afterwards bishop of Emly. Another Dominican Convent called "Saint Mary of Graces" still exists at Milan.

CHALICE OF YOUGHAL CONVENT.

convent were dispersed by the enemies of religion, the sacred vessels, vestments, and other religious objects, should be sent to the nearest community, that they might not be lost or desecrated. This regulation reasonably accounts for the existence of three objects

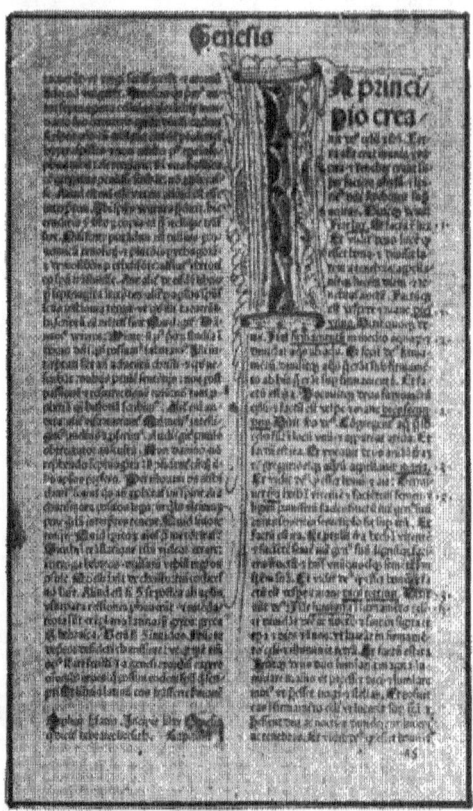

FACSIMILE PAGE OF BLACK-LETTER BIBLE.

of interest and veneration found by Father Russell in 1823, on his return to Ireland from Lisbon, in the old safe of Dominick Street, namely—the image of "Our Lady of Graces," the chalice of Youghal Convent, and an old black-letter copy of the Bible, on the front page of which are written the following words, showing its antiquity and authenticity :—" This Bible was printed at Strasburgh by Nicolas Pistoris, of Bonsheim, and Mark Remhardi, in the name of Nicolas Philippi, 1481, I.M."[82] On the chalice also is this inscription :—*Pertinet ad Conventum Deiparæ Gratiarum De Yeoghall*, 1632. " This chalice belongs to the convent of the Divine Mother of Graces of Youghal, 1632."

The following description of the chalice will be of interest to my readers:—"It rests on a hexagonal foot, the base being formed of six fan-shaped spandrels. Two of these are engraved with a conventional lily decoration, which so often occurs upon Cork chalices of the same period. The third space has the crucifixion, with the Redeemer's feet resting on a skull, and placed against the cross on each side are a spear and ladder. The three remaining spaces are plain and devoid of ornament. The knop is globular and is divided into six vesica-shaped spaces, and the cup springs from a rose of six petals, three of which are plain and three engraved to correspond with the ornamentation of the base and knop. The inscription surrounds the base; the extreme height of the chalice is 9 inches; the width of the cup is $3\frac{5}{8}$ inches, its height $3\frac{1}{8}$ inches; and the extreme width of the base measures $4\frac{3}{8}$ inches."

[82] I have been assured by Robert Day, Esq., J.P., a distinguished antiquarian, to whose kindness I am indebted for the description of the Youghal chalice, that when printing was first introduced it was not customary to insert a title page in books.

Castlelyons.
Convent of the Blessed Virgin Mary.

> "Sweet as the warbling of a bird,
> Sweet as a mother's voice;
> So sweet to me is that dear name!
> It makes my soul rejoice.
>
> Bright as the glittering stars appear,
> Bright as the moonbeams shine;
> So bright in my mind's eye is seen
> Thy loveliness divine.
>
> But I must view thee as thou art,
> Pleading with earnest prayer,
> Kneeling before God's mercy seat,
> Our advocate, most fair."
>
> "Name of Mary."

THE Friars Preachers owe their foundation in Castlelyons to John Barry, of the family of Barrymore, who built a church and convent for them in that town in the year 1307. Castlelyons is situated in the valley of the Bride, about three miles from Fermoy, It is asserted by Ware[83] that the house belonged not to the Dominicans, but to the Friars Minors. Various reasons, however, lead us to call in question this assertion. First it is certain that in 1644, ten years before

[83] *De Antiquitatibus Hibernicis*, published 1654.

Ware wrote on the subject, there were forty-three Dominican convents in Ireland.[84] In 1720 a Provincial Chapter, held in Dublin, refers in a very marked manner to the existence of these convents in the year 1644, but if a house of the Order did not then exist at Castlelyons, it would be difficult to understand that there was such a number of convents in the country. Moreover Wadding, O.S.F.,[85] the celebrated historian of his Order, makes no mention of a Franciscan convent being in Castlelyons at that time. In 1660, however, a house of the Friars Minors was opened in the town. A chapter held by them in Dublin in 1680 referred to the convent of Castlelyons as being amongst those places where no guardians could be appointed on account of the unsettled state of the times.[86]

In 1673, when the Cromwellian cruelties had fully ceased, the Provincial of the Irish Dominicans, Father Constantius O'Cuiffe, appointed William Barry prior of Castlelyons, at the request of Lord Barrymore, though a Protestant. He told the Provincial that according to the family records his ancestors had founded this convent for the Friars Preachers. The same nobleman, when James II. ascended the throne, gave the Prior full possession of the lands belonging to this religious foundation. This fact we have on the authority of O'Heyne, O.P., whose *Epilogus Chronol.*

[84] *Acts of General Chapter, held in Rome* 1656. *Hib. Dom.*, p. 291.
[85] He was born in 1588, and died 1657.
[86] *Archives of the Franciscan Fathers of Cork.*

Convent of Castlelyons.

appeared in 1706. He was at this time sixty years old, and acquainted with Fathers O'Cuiffe and Barry, from whom most probably he learned the facts which have been mentioned. Ware's mistake can be accounted for by saying that there may have been, as in other parts of Ireland, two convents at Castlelyons—one of the Franciscans, and the other of the Dominicans—and that as in Youghal both were introduced by the Fitzgeralds, so in the present case the two foundations owed their origin to the family of the Barrymores.

The lands belonging to this convent were granted at the time of the dissolution of religious houses to Richard Boyle, Lord Cork, who assigned them to his son-in-law, David Barry, the first Earl of Barrymore. In the reign of James II., as has been already said, the Dominicans regained possession of them, but in the year 1698, when the bishops and other dignitaries, as well as the regulars, were exiled from the kingdom, the property finally reverted to Lord Barrymore, and is still in the hands of the family.

In the year 1749 the ruins of the Castlelyons Convent, with the nave, choir, and bell-tower of the adjoining church, were seen by De Burgo,[87] and all these structures appear to be yet in the same condition, as can be inferred from the illustration which accompanies the account now brought to a close.

[87] *Hib. Dom.*, p. 292.

Glanworth.

Convent of the Holy Cross.

"O honoured cross, O beauteous tree,
In Eden's bowers was none like thee,
What glory may with thine compare,
The Lord, the King of Kings, to bear."

N a hill above the bank of the river Funcheon, which flows to the north-west of Glanworth, county Cork, the noble family of the Roches, who were proprietors of the town, established a convent of the Dominican Order. This distinguished family is of French origin, and was called "de la Roche." It traces its descent from Charlemagne and other kings of France, as likewise from the counts of Flanders. It also claims relationship to the kings of England through Elizabeth de Clare, the niece of Edward I., who being the widow of John de Burgo, father of William, the duke of Ulster, married Raphael de la Roche.[88]

Though many trustworthy writers [89] make express mention of this Dominican foundation, Charles Smith

---

[88] This account is taken from the genealogy of this family compiled in 1615 by Sir William Segar, commonly called "garter," and found in the *Heraldic Registry of London. Hib. Dom.*, p. 334.

[89] Ware, Harris, Alemand, O'Heyne, and Echard, O.P.

alone[90] gives as the date of its occurrence 1227. This, however, must have been a typographical error, for though the writer may have discovered this date in otherwise reliable manuscripts, it could not be the year in which the Dominicans first settled in Glanworth, as no mention is made of their existence there in the "Catalogue of the Convents in Ireland" drawn up by a member of the Order in 1300. It must have been therefore after this Catalogue had appeared that the Order was introduced.

The ruins of the church still exist, and they consist of the nave and chancel. Between them rises a low square tower, supported on four finely pointed arches. The windows, though square on the outside, are beautifully arched on the interior. Near the castle, the ancient seat of the Roches, which is situated just on the margin of the river, is a well dedicated to St. Dominic, which is held in great veneration by the peasantry.[91] Smith tells us that at his time a large concourse of people used to assemble every year at the well on the 4th August, the feast of St. Dominic, and that many tokens of miracles were to be seen on a beautiful tree overhanging the well.[92]

Father David Roche, who lived in the convent of Glanworth about the year 1640, was distinguished for

[90] *History of Cork*, vol. i., p. 351.

[91] The castle was occupied by Lord Fermoy in 1601, but forfeited by his descendant in 1641.—*Lewis' Topographical Dictionary*, vol. i., p. 655.

[92] *History of Cork*, 1750.

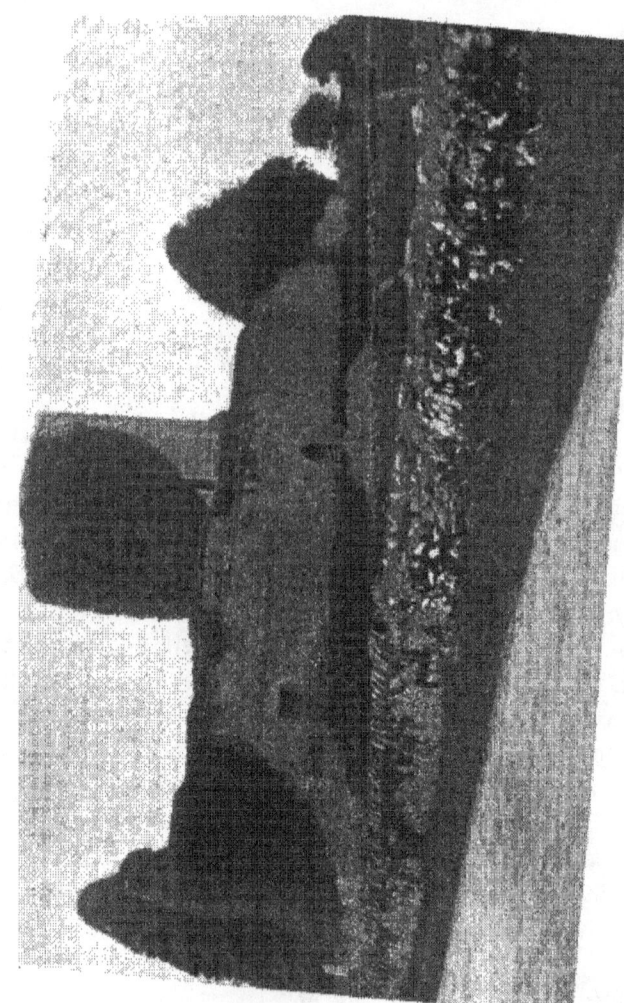

Convent of Glanworth.

his great virtue and learning, as well as eloquence and cultivated manners. He was esteemed as a man of great merit throughout the whole of Munster.[93] Another Dominican of this house, Father John Browne, was residing with James III. (commonly so called), as his confessor, and that of the Queen, Mary Clementine. He received the habit in the convent of Glanworth from a namesake, Father John Browne, who was a native of Galway, and Provincial of Ireland during the reign of James II.[94]

Besides these two illustrious men there were others affiliated to the Glanworth convent whose career is deserving of special notice.

Theobald Roche was master of studies in 1654 at Louvain. He held this position till the end of 1657, spreading around him the light of his extensive knowledge and the odour of his virtue.

Gerald Gibbon studied at Burgos, in Spain, and then returning to Ireland became remarkable for his great and persuasive eloquence. He was prior of the convent of Glanworth, his native town, as also in other parts of Munster. Having clothed many young aspirants with the habit of the Order, he was at length obliged to fly from his convent on account of the persecutions, and went to Belgium. He died a holy death in 1685.

Constantine O'Garavain having made his studies

---

[93] O'Heyne, o.p., *Epil. Chronol.*, quoted by *Hib. Dom.*, p. 615.
[94] *Idem*, p. 335.

with distinction in the convent of the Most Blessed Virgin of Athoca at Madrid, returned in 1673 to his native country, where he laboured most zealously

DOORWAY IN TOWER, CONVENT OF GLANWORTH.

amongst the people for twenty-six years, both in the pulpit and confessional. He received a large number into the Order, but was finally compelled to leave

Ireland in 1699, and go into Burgundy, in France. O'Heyne, the Dominican writer, who was intimately acquainted with Father O'Garavain from his childhood, described him as being "a man of the highest character, and of an exceedingly mild disposition."

John O'Brian, having completed his ecclesiastical course in Palencia, in Old Castile, was appointed lecturer of philosophy at the convent of Holy Cross, in Louvain, and also sub-prior and master of novices. He then went into Spain, but was, in 1686, elected prior of Louvain, where towards the end of the following year he was made sub-regent, and subsequently regent of studies. Having completed his office, he passed into Portugal. Whilst there engaged in teaching he was made master of theology. Then leaving Portugal he went to Viterbo, in Italy. Father O'Brian was not only distinguished for his great learning, but also for the holiness of his life.

Peter Hennessy, of the same convent of Glanworth, studied philosophy in Galway under the celebrated O'Heyne, and afterwards theology in Brittany. When ordained priest he was usually engaged as curate or vicar in some church in the town of Galway, and was an eloquent and impressive preacher.

There were two other Dominicans of Holy Cross, Glanworth, the account of whose career will, I think, interest our readers, were it only for the coincidence that they were both brothers, not only in religion, but also of the same family.

Father O'Garavain, having completed his collegiate

course with *eclat* in Spain, was desirous to return to Ireland, but his wishes were frustrated by the destructive and cruel war of William, Prince of Orange. Going, therefore, to La Rochelle, in France, he remained there for many years in the convent of his Order. He was remarkable for his rare virtue as a religious.

His brother left his native country, intending likewise to prosecute his studies in Spain, but was captured at sea by the Moors, and sold as a slave to an African prince. The daughter of this prince becoming greatly attached to him on account of his manly beauty, the father offered her in marriage to young Garavain on condition of his abandoning the faith of Christ and professing himself a Mahometan. But the good religious boldly refused not only to abjure his holy faith, but also to get married though he should still remain a Christian. The prince being unable to overcome his wonderful fortitude by favours or ill-treatment, handed him over to a Turkish pasha, with whom he remained faithful to his religion and the vows he had made to God.[95]

[95] *Epilogus Chronologicus.*—O'Heyne, O.P.

Conclusion.

I HAVE now brought to a close this "Historical Account" of the Dominicans of Cork city and county. I have shewn what they achieved since their arrival in the city in 1229, and likewise in Youghal, Castlelyons, and Glanworth, from the time of their respective foundations; how devoted they ever were to the call of duty, even when exposed to imprisonment or death. For more than six hundred and sixty years their succession amongst the people of Cork has never been interrupted, notwithstanding the persecutions to which they were subjected. But how is this fidelity and this marvellous steadfastness of purpose to be explained? Simply by that bond of brotherhood, or golden chain, the precious links of which consist of their three vows to God and His representatives. These promises imposed no galling shackles, but rather a light yoke, freeing them from all worldly ties, and forming them into a solid phalanx, ever ready to do battle with the enemies of religion and humanity. It is true their weapons, though honourable, did not always meet with the world's approval. To this, however, they were quite indifferent, for their principles were not of the world, but of Christ their

Master, who they did well to remember was always looked upon as a sign to be contradicted. Every friar preacher might with good reason have appropriated to himself that beautiful motto of Cardinal Newman, *Cor ad cor loquitur*—" Heart speaks to heart "—for each had in view the same objects and professed the same obligations as his brethren. He therefore well understood the aspirations of those whose sole ambition was to have but "one heart and one soul." Being men of intellect and extensive knowledge, they only aimed at " Truth," the standard of their Order; and recognizing that " Knowledge is power," they persevered in their undertakings, and boldly faced the attendant dangers, fully conscious that truth would in the end prevail.

We must likewise remember their strong and undying attachment to the Irish people, whose prospects, temporal and spiritual, they had at heart; nor turned they to right or left when the welfare of Ireland's sons and daughters was threatened, but rather endangered life itself in their efforts to save them from national degradation or hopeless despair. No wonder, then, that well-informed Protestants should defend them in their untiring exertions for Faith and Fatherland—the two objects with them uppermost, whether in distant lands or on their native soil.

Whilst, then, the members of religious orders are now-a-days regarded by some with contempt and distrust, might they not at least be allowed to enjoy that liberty of conscience which is the universal claim of this nineteenth century? Should they commit a crime against society, let them, like others, be punished rigorously. But when they are despoiled of liberty and deemed unworthy to live amongst their own people, simply because they profess to observe what is clearly prescribed in the Gospel as the more perfect state, can lovers of justice and fair-play blame the regular clergy for complaining that they are treated in an exceptionally harsh manner in being excluded from the benefits conferred on their fellow-Catholics by the Emancipation Act of 1829? The regulars are still inscribed on the Statute Book as outlaws and felons. Are those opprobrious epithets never to be erased, or are they to remain as a stigma against a nation that more than any other in the world makes profession of liberty and justice? Why should England, whose flag is thrown as a shield of protection over those subject to her sway, and whose cherished motto is *Fiat Justitia*, permit such a stain to disfigure her laws? Were these odious statutes generously and speedily abolished, a new era of religious freedom would dawn for Catholics, as with their priests, regular as well as secular, they could in future serve God without fear of molestation from those who do not profess their faith or understand their cherished traditions.

Appendix.

Three Important Occurrences.

TO bring the account of the Cork Dominicans up to the present date, 1896, it is necessary to leave on record three important occurrences.

The first was the election of the Very Rev. J. L. Hickey as Provincial. It took place in the Provincial Chapter held in St. Saviour's Priory, Dublin, on the 25th of April, 1896. Father Hickey having resided in Cork as Prior of St. Mary's or otherwise at various times, had become well known to the citizens, and won universal esteem. Before he was chosen Provincial he had been in Rome for a number of years as Prior of San Clemente, or Consultor of the Congregation of the Council, and "Qualificator" of the Holy Office. In whatever position he occupied he was invariably held in the highest regard by all with whom he came into contact.

The second occurrence was the expiration of the Very Rev. J. M. Moore's tenure of office as Prior. It terminated immediately after the Provincial Chapter. Only a short time elapsed when he was unanimously elected Prior of St. Mary's of the Rosary, Tallaght, county Dublin. Father Moore, on his departure from Cork, left behind him the most enduring sentiments of affection and regard on the part of the inmates of St. Mary's Priory, and a host of others outside the community.

He was succeeded in St. Mary's by the Very Rev. M. A. Keane, who was installed in his office on the 20th of June, to the great pleasure of the Dominicans, who hailed his arrival amongst them.

List of Deaths.

A list of deaths drawn up by Father B. T. Russell was found in one of his manuscript books, and as it comprises most of the time spent by the Dominicans either in Old Friary Lane or Dominick Street, the writer inserts it here:—

Obits.—St. Mary's, Cork.

Father Master Dominic Morrogh, whose signature is attached to the "approbation" of "De Burgo," *Hib. Dom.*, as "Theol. Magr.," died April 20th, 1759.

The second whose "approbation" is attached being Father "Joannes Franciscus Netterville, Ordinis Prædicatorum, S. Theologiæ Magister" [year not given].

Father Master Daniel O'Brien, 1780.
Father John O'Mahony (Trinity Sunday) June 3rd, 1787.
Father William Lonergan, August 15th, 1787.
Father Lewis Walshe, P.G., January 10th, 1792.
Father William Hanly, P.G., January 28th, 1793.
Father Michael Mead, P.G., June 1st, 1798.
Father Master John Sheahan, April 5th, 1800.
Father Master Antony Conway, August 3rd, 1802.
Father Richard Roche, Sæ. Thesæ. Præs., September 6th, 1805.
Father Eugene McCrohan, P.G., June 26th, 1811.
Father Patrick Lonergan, October 8th, 1819.
Father Master Denis Dean, June 18th, 1827.

(*From Directories of various dates.*)

Father Master John Nugent, 1820.
Father P. J. Robert O'Connel, 1837.
Very Rev. Patrick Hyacinth O'Loughlin, P.G., June 23rd, 1837.
Very Rev. John Lewis Savage.
Father Bartholomew Hyacinth Power, died in Australia, August 6th, 1864.

The following personal memorandum addressed to his brethren, and likewise in Father Russell's handwriting, was subjoined to the list of obits. :—

Amongst our benefactors remember in the suffrages of the Order Mary Letitia B——, Sister of Charity, who died in St. Vincent's Hospital, and was buried in the Sisters' Cemetery, Donnybrook. Recall again and again her holy life and liberality towards our Convent of St. Mary's, Cork. Amongst our friends of the secular clergy remember especially the Very Rev. Michael O. Sullivan, founder and vicar-general of the Vincentian Congregation of Missions in Cork.

The Rev. Maurice Walsh, P.P., of the Ovens, diocese of Cork.

The Rev. John Crowe, P.P., Carrigaline.(96)

(96) Many others should be held in grateful remembrance as benefactors by the Dominicans of Cork.

Letter of Invitation received by Father Leahy to be present at the Synod of Thurles.

The Very Rev. John Pius Leahy, provincial of the Dominican Order in Ireland, received the following document, printed in Latin, from the Most Rev. Dr. Paul Cullen, then archbishop of Armagh, on the 8th of August, 1850. A faithful translation of it is here given:—

"Paul, by the grace of God and the favour of the Apostolic See, archbishop of Armagh, primate of All Ireland, delegate of the Apostolic See, etc.

To our most illustrious and reverend brethren, the archbishops and bishops of Ireland, and all others who are bound to attend the National Synod, greeting in the Lord.

By our other letters, published on the thirtieth day of May, we summoned the Plenary Synod of Ireland, to be held at Thurles on the fifteenth day of August, the feast of the Assumption of the Most Blessed Virgin Mary. As, however, for grave reasons, it cannot be celebrated on the appointed day, by the same authority with which we convoked it, we defer and adjourn it to the twenty-second of the same month of August.

On that day, therefore, we ask and require in the Lord all archbishops and bishops and others obliged to attend, to assemble in the same city on the aforesaid twenty-second day of August, in order to inaugurate the Synod with becoming solemnity. Meanwhile, we earnestly desire that God be again and again implored to deign to infuse into our minds the spirit of His wisdom, so that by His divine assistance we may be able to accomplish by fitting means those things which are right and avoid all evils.

Given at Drogheda, on the sixth day of August, in the year eighteen hundred and fifty.

N.B.—A preliminary meeting will be held on the twenty-first."
The Very Rev. Mr. Leahy.

MEMORIAL OF THE REGULARS OF IRELAND ADDRESSED TO MEMBERS OF BOTH HOUSES OF PARLIAMENT, APRIL, 1829.

Drawn up by REV. JOHN P. LEAHY, O.S.D., afterwards Bishop of Dromore.

(*See* page 64.)

To the Wisdom of the Members of both Houses of Parliament, the following considerations are respectfully submitted on behalf of the Regular Clergy professing the Roman Catholic Religion in Ireland.

This small and unprotected portion of his Majesty's subjects have learned that a Bill is now in progress through Parliament containing clauses intended for their gradual but certain extinction. Conscious of their own innocence, they most humbly deprecate a measure injurious to their reputation, and, in their humble opinion, wholly unmerited.

1st. They have taken the Oath of Allegiance, and exerted themselves to disseminate, as widely as their influence extended, the principles of loyalty and good morals. One of their brethren (ARTHUR O'LEARY) was the first to vindicate that Oath of Allegiance, and at a time when the French, then at war with this country, were presumed to be landed in this Kingdom, he, by the force, frequency, and eloquence of his Addresses, confirmed the Common People in their allegiance, and attached them unalterably to the Throne. In thus discharging his duty, he only went before, but scarcely surpassed in zeal his less gifted Brethren.

2nd. In the year 1756, when a motion, unfavourable to the Regular Clergy, was made in the Irish House of Commons, the generality of the Kingdom thought it cruel to harass or oppress them. In the year 1782 a similar motion was attended with a like result. These humble men of retired habits, therefore, trust that in the second quarter of the nineteenth century, when the spirit of toleration has gained such universal ascendancy, illiberal enactments, which were rejected at a less enlightened period, will not be adopted. Even in the Turkish dominions, at Constantinople, Jerusalem, and other places, the Religious Orders, now threatened with proscription in Ireland, are tolerated.

3rd. In the Regular Institutes, as existing in this country, there is nothing, it is presumed, which would seem to call for their destruction. The Members of these Institutes, like the other Roman Catholic Clergy, derive their subsistence from the voluntary contributions of the faithful, and their slender income is given in exchange for the necessaries of life. They are governed by a Superior of their own Body, who is always a native of this kingdom, and the most conspicuous among them for his prudence, learning, and piety. He has the power of correction; and, in case of omission on his part, that power devolves to the Bishop, without whose licence Regular or Secular Clergymen do not preach or perform any Ministerial Function. Thus, their internal economy relates only to their private conduct, whilst their public ministry, subject to the same inspection, correction, or control, as that of the Secular Clergy, is employed to promote the order of Society, to inculcate the principles of Morality, and in numberless instances, to bestow an excellent and gratuitous education on the poor.

4th. Should any illustrious Member imagine that their suppression is acceptable to the Catholic Laity, they most humbly request a supension of judgment until they can produce proofs to the contrary. The opinion of a few, if any there be, cannot counterbalance the voice of millions; and a body of men expect from the Wisdom of the Legislature the justice which a single Judge would not refuse a Culprit, namely, that of being heard in his defence before sentence is passed. To prove that they have not deserved punishment, they refer with gratitude to the Petitions to be presented to Parliament in their favour by those best acquainted with their conduct.

5th. The prospective nature of the clauses affecting Regulars in the Roman Catholic Relief Bill would appear to imply, either that the liberty which a Roman Catholic inherits from the Gospel, of serving God in the manner he deems most conformable to his conscience, should be restrained; or that the principles and institutions of the Regular Clergy of the Kingdom are subversive of the peace and order of society. If upon examination the latter can be discovered, immediate punishment, not indulgence, should be awarded them.

6th. Nor do the reasons alleged for their extinction appear well founded. Those adduced by a Right Honorable Member of the House of Commons on moving for a Committee, were (as is most respectfully submitted) altogether groundless, and must have originated in a misconception of Religious Institutions, or in impressions, resulting from insidious misrepresentations: for,

> It is not correct to state, "that they owe no allegiance, save to a Foreign Superior," because they know, and are convinced, that their Religious Obedience does not in the slightest degree conflict or interfere with that full and perfect allegiance which, confirmed by oath, they owe and pay only to His Most Gracious Majesty, KING GEORGE IV.

> It is not correct to state, "that they are unnecessary to the free exercise of the Roman Catholic Religion." That Religion contemplates the practice of certain virtues, confirmed by Vow, as tending to the greatest perfection of a Christian life, and where the making of such Vows is prohibited under penalties, now inflicted only on Felons, the exercise of that religion cannot be free.

> It is not correct to state, "that the Suppression of Regular Orders has been called for by the Protestant portion of the Nation." The Bishops of England have not demanded it; neither have the Bishops of Ireland. No such enactment has been required in a single Petition presented on behalf of any of the Universities. Such demands may have been made, but they have proceeded from persons unacquainted with the nature and character of Religious Institutions, and were founded on groundless prejudices. Do they deserve the attention of a statesman? The very places from which

Petitions against the Regulars proceeded were precisely those in which not a single Regular existed. Their destruction was not required by Lancashire, Dublin, or Cork, districts wherein the Regular Clergymen are most numerous. They, therefore, confidently hope that Honorable Members will not suffer an unoffending Body to be most grievously injured and finally destroyed, merely to dissipate the misconceptions of uninformed men.

It is not correct to state, that the clauses referred to "will not affect the present Members of Regular Orders." A certain number in each House is necessary to perform the clerical duties therein established; should the number be diminished the religious wants of the Public will not be supplied, nor the surviving Members of the Institution be furnished with support; thus would these latter be destined to suffer more than the ordinary infirmities and helplessness of old age.

7th. In conclusion, they respectfully call your attention to the impolicy of embodying in a Relief Bill, framed for the express purpose of producing general satisfaction, the severe penalties consequent on a misdemeanour, and these to be inflicted on persons whose only crime would be that of serving God in the best manner their consciences might dictate. Is this the freedom we deem our birthright? Or is it justice to stigmatise a body of men without affording to them the means of vindicating their conduct? or to punish as criminals freeborn subjects whose loyalty and allegiance stand unimpeachable and unimpeached? THE REGULAR CLERGY PROFESSING THE ROMAN CATHOLIC RELIGION IN IRELAND cannot cease to hope that the Senators and Counsellors of a most Gracious King, in a free country, will not sanction clauses so uncalled for, so impolitic, and so severe.

IMPORTANT CHARGE CONCERNING THE CATHOLIC RELIGIOUS COMMUNITIES, DELIVERED IN THE ROLLS COURT, DUBLIN, ON THE 3RD OF NOVEMBER, 1864.

James Richard Simms, petitioner ; Jeremiah Quinlan and John Egan, Executors of Michael John Simms, deceased, and Bridget Simms, respondent ; and the Court of Chancery Regulation Act, 1850, sec. 15.

Decision of MASTER OF ROLLS (drawn up and corrected by himself.)

The Master of the Rolls proceeded to deliver judgment in this case, as follows :—

A motion has been made in this case, on behalf of the Rev. Robert White and the Rev. Bartholomew Thomas Russell, by way of appeal against the order of William Brooke, Esq., the Master in this matter, bearing date the 13th January, and signed 4th March, 1864; and a motion has also been made, by way of appeal against the said order, on behalf of the Rev. Thomas Conway. The petitioner, James Richard Simms, is the residuary legatee in the will of Michael John Simms; the respondents, Jeremiah Quinlan and John Egan, are his executors. The questions which arise are—first, whether the bequest in the will of the testator, Michael John Simms (called by mistake Matthew James Simms in the Master's order), to the Rev. Robert White and the Rev. Bartholomew T. Russell, and the bequest in the said will to the Rev. Thomas Conway, are void; secondly, If void, are they bequests for charitable purposes, and should they be carried out *cy pres ?* The part of the Master's order appealed from is as follows :—"Having regard to the statute of the 10th George IV., c. 7 (the Roman Catholic Relief Act), I declare the bequests in the will of the testator, Matthew James Simms, to the Rev. Robert White and the Rev. Bartholomew Thomas Russell; and of £500 to the Rev. Thomas Conway, as trustee for the benefit of the Order of the Dominican Friars respectively, null and void; and being so void by the statute law, the sums thereby bequeathed form part of the residuary fund of the said testator." The name Matthew James in the Master's order is a mistake for Michael John. I shall first consider the bequest to the Rev. Robert White and the Rev. Bartholomew Thomas Russell. The bequest is in these words :—" I bequeath £500 to the Rev. Robert White and the Rev. Bartholomew Thomas Russell, of St. Saviour's Roman Catholic Church, Dublin, or the survivor of them, to be applied as they shall deem best for the maintenance and education of two priests of the Order of Saint Dominic in Ireland." The petitioner, James Richard Simms (who was, as I have already stated, residuary legatee in the said will), filed his discharge on the 3rd March, 1863, to the charge of Jeremiah Quinlan and John Egan, the executors of the said will; and the said discharge states, amongst other things, as follows :—"That by the will of the said Michael John Simms, the testator bequeathed £500 to the Rev. Robert White and the Rev. Bartholomew Thomas Russell, and the survivor of them, to be applied as they should deem best for the education and maintenance of two priests of the Order of Saint Dominic in Ireland; and dischargeant, as residuary legatee of the said Michael John Simms, and interested as such in setting aside the said legacy, avers and charges that the said Order of Saint Dominic in Ireland [for the education and maintenance of two priests, of which order the said legacy is so bequeathed as aforesaid] is a religious order, community, or society of the Church of Rome, resident in the United Kingdom, and bound by monastic vows ; and dischargeant avers that said order consists either of persons who became and were admitted members thereof since the 23rd of April, 1829 [the date on which the Roman Catholic Relief Act came into operation], or who, being then members of the same, did not deliver to the clerk of the peace of the county where they were then residing the notice or statement required by the provisions of the statutes in that behalf; and dischargeant avers that the said order is an illegal society, and that the said sum of £500 was bequeathed for the maintenance and benefit of said order, and for the education of priests to be members of the said order, and dischargeant therefore submits that the said legacy is void for illegality, and also for uncertainty." The said Rev. Robert White, by the name of Robert Augustin White, and the Rev. Bartholomew Thomas Russell, filed their charge on the 5th May, 1863, and submit to the court that the legacy bequeathed to them is not void on any of the grounds stated in the discharge of the petitioner, and their charge proceeds thus:—"These chargeants admit that they are members of the Order of Saint Dominic, and priests of that order, and that the Order of Saint Dominic is an order of the Roman Catholic Church, bound by religious and monastic vows; but chargeants altogether deny that the said order consists either of persons who became, and were admitted, members thereof since the 13th day of April, 1829 [this is the date of the Royal assent, but the act did not come into operation for ten days—*i.e.*, until the 23rd of April, 1829], or who, being then members of the same did not deliver to the clerk of the peace for the county wherein they were then residing, the notice or statement required by the provisions of statute in that behalf, for chargeants say that they themselves were respectively members of the order prior to the 13th of April, 1829, and that each of them duly delivered to the clerk of the peace of the county of the city of Dublin, on or about the month of October, 1829, the notice or statement required by the 28th section of the statute of the 10th George IV., c. 7, and the schedule annexed to the said act. And chargeants further say that there are in Ireland a considerable number of persons members of the said order, who were members thereof before the passing of the said act, and who delivered to the clerks of the peace of their respective counties such notice or statement as by the said act required. And chargeants submit, as matter of law, that the said bequest to chargeants, upon the trust aforesaid, is not invalidated by the terms of the statute; and further, that even if the court should be of opinion that it would be illegal to apply the amount of the said bequest for the benefit of any members of the said order, becoming such after the passing of the said act, yet that is competent for chargeants legally to apply

CORK CITY AND COUNTY.   153

the same for the benefit of the said members of the said order, who were such previous to the passing of the said act." The chargeants then submit that if the bequest was illegal, the amount of the legacy should be applied by the court, *cy pres*, for such legal charitable purposes as would most nearly approximate to the objects specified by the testator, and that if the bequest is illegal, a scheme should be settled by the court. A discharge has been filed by the petitioner to the charge of the said Rev. Robert White and the Rev. Bartholomew Thomas Russell, and the petitioner submits that the legacy to them is void, even though they should establish the statements therein by evidence. An affidavit was made by the petitioner in support of his statements, which affidavit was filed on the 26th of June, 1863. I shall refer to that affidavit more particularly when considering the case of the legacy to the Rev. Mr. Conway. It has been contended, on the part of the appellants (the Rev. Robert White and the Rev. B. T. Russell), that they are entitled under the will of the testator to apply the legacy of £500 "as they shall deem best for the education and maintenance of two priests of the Order of Saint Dominic in Ireland," and that it would not be illegal to apply the £500 to the education and maintenance of such priests of the order as were such at the passing of 10 George IV., c. 7, and who complied with the terms of the statute, and that therefore the legacy is valid. I am of opinion that that is not a reasonable construction of the bequest. The priests of the order who were so in 1829 were advanced in life at the date of the will (15th November, 1861), which was thirty-two years after the passing of the statute, and I do not think that the testator can be presumed to have intended that the £500 should be applied exclusively, if at all, for the education of priests of the Order of Saint Dominic, who must, at the date of the will, have been between fifty and sixty years of age. If not, the bequest is void.(97) I do not, however, concur with the Master, who by his order states that the bequest is "void by the Statute Law"; and

(97) Sir B. Read's case referred to in 4 *Reports*, 113.

the necessity of deciding whether the bequest is void as being
contrary to the policy of the law, or void by the express terms
of the statute, is that if a charitable bequest is void by the express
enactment of a statute, the bequest cannot be carried out *cy pres;*
but if the bequest is void as being contrary to the policy of the law
the bequest may, according to the weight of authority, be carried
out *cy pres.* There is no provision in the statute of George IV.,
c. 7, making a bequest in favour of persons bound by monastic
vows void. The 15th section of the 7 and 8 Vic., c. 97, contains
the following proviso:—" Provided always that nothing herein
mentioned shall be construed to render lawful any donation,
devise, or bequest to or in favour of any religious order, community, or society of the Church of Rome bound by monastic or
religious vows, prohibited by an act passed in the 10th year of
the reign of King George IV., entitled 'An Act for the Relief of his
Majesty's Roman Catholic Subjects, to or in favour of any member or members thereof.'" But it appears to me that the latter
statute carried the matter no farther than the 10th George IV.,
c. 7; and it was, I apprehend, only intended by the Charitable
Bequests Act to exclude from its operation bequests void, as
being contrary to the policy of the 10th George IV. It is
necessary, therefore, to consider (there being no express provision in the latter Act making a gift or bequest in favour of
persons bound by monastic vows void) whether such bequest is
void as against the policy of the statute. Previous to the Toleration Act dissent was neither recognised nor permitted. In the
case of the King *v.* Larwood (*Lord Raymond,* p. 30), it is laid
down that "time out of mind there was a discipline established
in the Church of England which all persons were obliged to
observe—by the canon law before the Reformation, and since
the Reformation by the statutes of Edward VI. and Elizabeth;
so that the law took no notice of such persons as Dissenters
before the act of the first William and Mary," the Toleration
Act. Thus, previously to the Reformation every one was, or
was supposed to be, a Roman Catholic; and from the Act of
Uniformity to the Toleration Act, every one was, or was sup-

posed to be, a member of the Church of England or Ireland, dissent being only connived at, but not recognised by law. The Toleration Act, first William and Mary [English], and 6 Geo. I., c. 5 [Irish], to a certain extent recognised dissent, but excluded Roman Catholics from the benefit of the enactment. The English Act, 31 Geo. III., c. 32, and the Irish Act, 33 Geo. III., c. 21, sec. 11, which provided that a Roman Catholic should not be subject to any penalty for not attending Divine service in the parish church, to a very limited extent gave toleration to the Roman Catholic Church.(98) Prior to the Reformation gifts or bequests for the promotion of doctrines opposed to the Roman Catholic religion, or to support ministers not of the Roman Catholic Church, would have been void, as opposed to the then policy of the law. After the Reformation, and Act of Uniformity, gifts or bequests for the promotion of doctrines opposed to the then Established religion, or for the support of Roman Catholic priests would have been void as contrary to the policy of the law. After the Toleration Act the law was altered as to Protestant Dissenters. As to Roman Catholics, I shall have to consider the statutes relaxing the penal laws. While the penal laws were in force a gift for the maintenance of Roman Catholic priests was decided to be superstitious and invalid.(99) So a bequest to be applied to such purposes as the superioress of a convent or her successor should deem most expedient was held to be void.(100) So a bequest of legacies to several Roman Catholic establishments in foreign countries and in these kingdoms were held to be void—viz., to each superior for the time being of the Benedictine Monks of the Southern or Northern provinces [an establishment in England], to the English Black Nuns at Paris, to the establishment of the Benedictine Nuns at Cambray, to the English Benedictine Monks of —— in Lorraine; to J. Bolton, for the maintenance of a Roman Catholic minister, for ever, were

(98) Evans v. Cassidy, 11 *Irish Equity Reports*, 249-250.
(99) Gates v. Jones, cited 2 *Vernon*, 266.
(100) Smart v. Prujean, 6 *Vesey*, 567.

held to be void.(101) So in Cary v. Abbott, 7 *Vesey*, 490, decided
in the year 1802, a bequest for the purpose of educating and
bringing up poor children in the Roman Catholic faith, was held
to be illegal—such bequest was void, as being contrary to the
then policy of the law, and not by reason of any provision by
statute making it void. With regard to Protestant dissenters,
prior to the Toleration Act, gifts in favour of their places of worship, ministers, or schools, were invalid, as being superstitious
—that is, as tending to promote doctrines contrary to those of
the Established religion.(102) It is perfectly clear, therefore, in
my opinion, that prior to the relaxation of the penal laws against
Roman Catholics, the bequest in this case to the Rev. Robert
White and the Rev. B. T. Russell, to be applied as they shall
deem best for the education and maintenance of two priests of
the Order of Saint Dominic in Ireland, would have been invalid
as contrary to the policy of the law. Although a bequest for the
maintenance and education of two secular priests of the Roman
Catholic Church would have been invalid prior to the relaxation
of the penal laws, yet such bequest would now be valid, having
regard to the provisions of the 10 Geo. IV., c. 7. The question,
however, is whether the bequest to the Rev. Robert White and
the Rev. B. T. Russell, to be applied as they shall deem best for
the education and maintenance of two priests of the Order of
Saint Dominic in Ireland is valid, that order being bound by
monastic vows, and the priests of the order being monks.
Mr. Brewster has referred to several statutes prior to the
10 George IV., c. 7, to show what the policy of this law was as to
the regular clergy, prior to the passing of that act ; and the
enactment of the 9 William III., c. 1 ; 2 Anne, c. 3 ; 2 Anne,
c. 7 ; 8 Anne, c. 3, sec. 16 and 31 ; 21 and 22 George III., c. 24,
sec. 5, are important to establish what was the policy. Was that
policy altered, so far as the regular clergy were concerned, by
the 10 George IV., c. 7 ?

(101) See De Garcia v. Lawson—Note to 4 *Vesey, jun.*, 2nd edition, 433.
(102) *Tudor's Law of Charitable Trusts*, 20.

CORK CITY AND COUNTY.   157

The 28th section of that statute is as follows :—

"And whereas Jesuits and members of other religious orders, communities, or societies of the Church of Rome, bound by monastic or religious vows, are resident within the United Kingdom, and it is expedient to make provision for the gradual suppression and final prohibition of the same therein; be it therefore enacted, that every Jesuit and every member of any other religious order, community, or society of the Church of Rome, bound by monastic or religious vows, who at the time of the commencement of the act shall be within the United Kingdom, shall, within six calendar months after the commencement of this act, deliver to the clerk of the peace of the county or place where such person shall reside, or to his deputy, a notice or statement in the form and containing the particulars required to be set forth in the schedule of this act annexed; which notice or statement such clerk of the peace or his deputy shall preserve and register amongst the records of such county or place, without any fee, and shall forthwith transmit a copy of such notice or statement to the Chief Secretary of the Lord Lieutenant, or other chief governor or governors of Ireland, if such person shall reside in Ireland, or if in Great Britain, to one of his Majesty's principal Secretaries of State; and in case any person shall offend in the premises, he shall forfeit and pay to his Majesty, for every calendar month during which he shall remain in the United Kingdom without having delivered such notice or statement as is hereinbefore required, the sum of £50."

The 29th section is as follows :—" And be it further enacted, that if any Jesuit or member of any such religious order, community, or society as aforesaid, shall, after the commencement of this act, come into this realm, he shall be deemed and taken to be guilty of a misdemeanour, and being thereof lawfully convicted, shall be sentenced and ordered to be banished from the United Kingdom for the term of his natural life."

The 33rd section enacts, "That in case any Jesuit or member of any such religious order, community, or society as aforesaid, shall, after the commencement of this act, within any part of the United Kingdom, admit any person to become a regular ecclesiastic, or brother, or member of any such religious order, community, or society, or be aiding or consenting thereto, or shall administer or cause to be administered, or be aiding or assisting in the administration or taking any oath, vow, or engagement purporting or intended to bind the person taking the same to the rules, ordinances, or ceremonies of such religious order, community, or society, every person offending in the premises in England or Ireland shall be deemed guilty of a misdemeanor, and in Scotland shall be punished by fine and imprisonment.

"34. And be it further enacted, that in case any person shall, after the commencement of this act, within any part of this United Kingdom, be admitted or become a Jesuit, or brother or member of any other such religious order, community, or society as aforesaid, such person shall be deemed and taken to be guilty of misdemeanor, and being thereof lawfully convicted, shall be sentenced and ordered to be banished from the United Kingdom for the term of his natural life.

"35. And be it further enacted, that in case any person sentenced and ordered to be banished under the provisions of this act, shall not depart from the United Kingdom within thirty days after the pronouncing of such sentence and order, it shall be lawful for his Majesty to cause such person to be conveyed to such place out of the United Kingdom as his Majesty, by the advice of his Privy Council, shall direct.

"36. And be it further enacted, that if any offender, who shall be so sentenced and ordered to be banished in manner aforesaid, shall, at the end of three calendar months from the time such sentence and order hath been pronounced, be at large within any part of the United Kingdom, without some lawful cause, every such offender being so at large as aforesaid, on being thereof lawfully convicted, shall be transported to such a place as shall be appointed by his Majesty for the term of his natural life."

I am of opinion, having regard to the sections of the said statutes of the 10 George IV., c. 7, to which I have referred,

that any bequest for the education and maintenance of regular priests of an order bound by monastic vows, who have become such since the passing of the statute, is invalid, being contrary to the policy of the law. There is, however, no express provision in the act making the bequest void. I have already stated that I do not consider it to be a reasonable construction of the bequest, and having regard to the date of the will (15th November, 1861) that it was to be applied exclusively for the benefit of the monks who were such on the 23rd of April, 1829, the date on which the act came into operation. If not, the bequest was void.[103] If the bequest was void, as being contrary to the policy of the law, but not void by the express provision of the statute, the next question which arises is, whether the bequest should be carried out *cy pres*. That question is one of difficulty. If a bequest is void under the express provision of a statute it will not be carried out *cy pres*.[104] However, when there is a charitable bequest, which is invalid as being contrary to the policy of the law, the bequest is applied *cy pres*. In Cary *v.* Abbott, 7 *Vesey*, 490, the bequest there (which would now be valid) was for the purpose of bringing up poor children in the Roman Catholic religion. The bequest was decided to be illegal, being contrary to the then policy of the law. The Master of the Rolls (Sir W. Grant), in giving judgment, said :—
"The consequence of the disposition being void, if authority was out of the question, would be an intestacy; that the gift, being so void, must be considered as no gift. But this is contradicted by authorities without number. According to them, whenever a testator is disposed to be charitable, in his own way and upon his own principles, we are not to content ourselves with disappointing his intention if disapproved by us; but we are to make him charitable in our way and upon our principles ; if once we discover in him any charitable intention, that is sup-

(103) See Sir B. Read's case, referred to 4 Reports, 113.

(104) 1 *Jarman on Wills*, 3rd edition, 225; *Tudor on Charitable Trusts*, 90, 273 ; Middleton *v.* Cater, 4 *B.C.C.* 409 ; Chapman *v.* Brown, 6 *Vesey*, 404.

posed to be so liberal as to take in objects not only within his intention, but wholly adverse to it, it is not for me to overturn the settled law and practice, according to which charitable bequests are void, as to one object, may be appropriated to another." So in Muggeridge *v.* Thackwell, 7 *Vesey,* 75, it was laid down by Lord Eldon that, where a gift denotes a charitable intention, but the object to which the exercise of it is applied is against the policy of the law (as in the case of a gift to superstitious uses), the court would lay hold of the charitable intention, and execute it for the purpose of establishing some charity agreeably to the law, in the room of that contrary to it. The case of the Attorney-General *v.* Vint, 3 *De Gex and Smale,* 704, appears to have been decided on the same principle. In *Shelford on the Law of Mortmain and Charitable Uses,* p. 99, it is thus laid down:—" When a devise is to a superstitious use made void by statute, or to a charity void by the statute 9 George II., c. 36, the land or fund will belong to the heir-at-law, or next of kin; but where it is in itself a charity, but the mode in which it is to be applied cannot by the law of England take effect, as for promoting a religion contrary to that established by law, then the Crown, by sign-manual directed to the Attorney-General, may give orders to what charitable purpose it shall be applied." Mr. Shelford then referred to Cary *v.* Abbott, which I have cited, in which the court declared the bequest of the residue to be void, but directed it to be applied to such use as the king should appoint by sign-manual. The same direction was given where money was directed to be applied in teaching the Jewish Law.[105] The question then arises, is the bequest to the Rev. R. White and the Rev. B. T. Russell a charitable bequest? I apprehend that a bequest for the benefit of ministers of any denomination of Christians is a charitable bequest.[106] It is now necessary to advert to the ground upon which the Master has

[105] Da Costa *v.* De Paz, *Ambler,* 228; 2 *Swanston,* 487. De Garcia *v.* Lawson; 4, *Vesey,* 433, 2nd edition; 1, *Mer,* 100.

[106] 1, *Jarman on Wills,* 193; *Tudor on Charitable Trusts,* p. 10; *Shelford on the Law of Mortmain and Charitable Trusts,* ed. 1836, p. 73.

decided that the bequest to the Rev. Robert White and the Rev. B. T. Russell cannot be carried out *cy pres*. The Master referred to the passage of Lord Hardwicke's judgment, in De Costa *v.* De Paz, *Ambler*, 288, that "When the devise is to a superstitious use, and made void by statute, or to a charity, and made void by the Statute of Mortmain, then it should belong to the heir-at-law or next of kin. But where it is in itself a charity, but the mode in which it is to be deposed is such that by the law of England it cannot take effect, as in the present case, promoting a religion contrary to the Established one, then the Crown, by sign-manual directed to the Attorney-General, may give orders what charitable manner it shall be disposed." The Master's judgment then proceeds thus:—" That passage is badly expressed. What, no doubt, Lord Hardwicke said, and what he has always been understood to have meant [107] was to draw a distinction between a gift void by statute, and one which, offending against no statute, was forbidden by the *lex non scripta.*" The Master then adds:—"As I shall have frequent occasion to refer to this distinction, it will be convenient to call it Lord Hardwicke's rule." The Master then refers to cases which, he considers, illustrate Lord Hardwicke's rule, as he understands it; but which, with great respect to the Master, appear to me to be opposed to the interpretation he has put on Lord Hardwicke's words.—Gates *v.* Jones 2 Vernon is thus stated in the Report— "Gates *v.* Jones: case in the Exchequer, affirmed in the House of Lords, where a charity was given to maintain Popish priests applied to other uses by the king, and not to turn to the benefit of the heir." The Master refers to the argument of counsel in Cary *v.* Abbott, to show that that case "is not to be found." Sir W. Grant, however, acted upon it in Cary *v.* Abbott. If Gates *v.* Jones be correctly reported, it is an authority against the Master's view. A gift to maintain Roman Catholic priests was, of course, perfectly legal by the common law. Such bequest became illegal by the effect of the Act of Uniformity, and

[107] See Lord Eldon's words, 7 *Vesey*, 46, 47, and Sir Wm. Grant's words, same volume, 495.

the penal laws against the Roman Catholics. There was no express enactment making gifts for the maintenance of Roman Catholic priests void, but it was clearly contrary to the policy of the statute law under which the Protestant Church was established. So in Cary v. Abbott, 7 , 590, the *Vesey* bequest was for the purpose of educating and bringing up poor children in the Roman Catholic faith—that would have been a perfectly valid bequest by the common law when the Roman Catholic religion was the Established religion. It became invalid by the operation of the Act of Uniformity and the penal laws against Roman Catholics. But there was no express enactment against a bequest for the educating of poor children in the Roman Catholic faith. The bequest, however, was against the policy of the statute law, and therefore invalid, but the bequest, being a charitable bequest, was carried out *cy pres*. The case of Da Costa v. De Paz was, no doubt, the case of a bequest for advancing the Jewish religion, and would have been invalid prior to the Reformation, as being contrary to the policy of the common law, but it was invalid as contrary to the policy of the statute law under which the Protestant religion had become the Established religion. So Lord Eldon laid down in Muggeridge v. Thackwell, that where a gift denotes a charitable intention, but the object to which the exercise of it is applied as against the policy of the law, as in the case of a gift to superstitious uses, the court would lay hold of the charitable intention and execute it for the purpose of establishing some charity agreeably to the law, in the room of that contrary to it. So the case of the Attorney-General v. Vint, 3 *De Gex. v. Small*, 704, is contrary to the view taken by the Master, as in that case the bequest was contrary to the policy of the statute law and not contrary to the policy of the common law. The result of the case appears to be this :—If a charitable gift or bequest is *expressly* made void by statute (as in case of the English Mortmain Act), the bequest will not be carried out *cy pres*. Secondly, if a charitable bequest is invalid, as being contrary to the policy of the common law or statute law, it will in general be carried out *cy pres*. Thirdly, if the testator shews an intention not of general charity, but to give to some particular institution in some particular place, and such intention cannot be carried out, the court will not hold that the gift is applicable to charity generally, it will fail altogether. Applying those principles to the appeal of the Rev. R. White and the Rev. B. T. Russell, I am of opinion that the bequest to the Rev. R. White and the Rev. B. T. Russell was a charitable bequest, but was invalid, being contrary to the policy of the 10 George IV., c. 7; but that it was not contrary to any express provision contained in that act. Secondly, being contrary to the policy of that act, the bequest is to be carried out *cy pres*. Thirdly, I am of opinion that the Wheatley Church case, and the decision of Lord Chancellor Blackburne in Carbery *v.* Cox, have no application to the bequest to the Rev. R. White and the Rev. B. T. Russell. Fourthly, the bequest should, in my opinion, be carried out under the sign-manual, and not by the court. The case of Muggeridge *v.* Thackwell, I think, establishes that, although there is some conflict in the cases. The case of West *v.* Shuttleworth, 2 *M. & K.*, 698, and cases of that class, have no application. Lord Cottenham, in giving judgment, said, with respect to bequests for masses, that there was nothing of charity in their object. The intention was not to benefit the parish, or to support the chapel, but to secure a supposed benefit for the testatrix herself.

With respect to the appeal by the Rev. Patrick Thomas Conway, the bequest to him was in these words:—"I bequeath £500 to the Rev. Patrick Thomas Conway, of St. Mary's Priory, Cork, Roman Catholic clergyman." No trust appears on the will, but there was a secret trust disclosed to the Rev. Mr. Conway by the testator in his lifetime; and if that trust was invalid the bequest is invalid.[108] The discharge of the petitioner to the charge of the executors alleged that the Rev. Thomas Conway was a member of the Order of Saint Dominic, and that is not denied; and the said discharge further stated that the said legacy to the Rev. Thomas Conway was in trust for the sole use and benefit of the

---

[108] Tee *v.* Ferris, 2 *Kay & J.*

members of the Order of Saint Dominic, and was void. The
Rev. P. T. Conway, by his charge, states—" That chargeant has
read that portion of the petitioner's discharge in this matter,
which impeaches the said bequest to this chargeant on the
ground that the said legacy was left to this chargeant upon
trust, that he would take and apply same for the maintenance
and support, or for the use and benefit of the members of the
Order of Saint Dominic resident in the United Kingdom, and
chargeant saith that no trust, save as hereinafter mentioned, was
imposed upon chargeant in relation to the said bequest—that is
to say, that he, the testator, had a conversation with chargeant,
who informed him that he had bequeathed, or would bequeath,
to chargeant the sum of £500, and that the said sum was, or
would be, so bequeathed to chargeant, to be applied in or
towards the redemption of the rent to which the church in Cork
with which this chargeant is connected was subject; and chargeant saith he does not remember the precise words used by the
said testator, but they were to the above effect. And chargeant
saith that the church with which chargeant, as a Roman Catholic
clergyman, is connected, is the Roman Catholic church or chapel
known as Saint Mary's Church, on Pope's Quay, in the city of
Cork, and that the said church is held by certain clergymen as
trustees thereof, subject to a yearly rent of £60 or thereabouts,
and chargeant submits that the said trust for redeeming the said
rent is a perfectly valid trust, and that the petitioner is not entitled by law to have the said bequest to chargeant set aside."
The petitioner has filed a discharge to the charge of the Rev.
T. P. Conway, which states that—"With regard to the third and
fourth paragraphs of said charge, petitioner refers to such proofs
as to the truth of the statements therein as the said chargeant
may make, and petitioner charges that the said church therein
referred to is a church belonging to said Order of Dominican
Monks, whereof the said chargeant is a member, and is maintained and kept by them and for their use and benefit as such
members of the said order, and for the exercise of their calling
and occupations as such members as aforesaid of said order, and

petitioner submits that the alleged trust for the redemption of the head rent of said church so used, attended, and occupied by the members of the said order, in the exercise of their calling as members of the said order, is one for their own use and benefit, and is therefore illegal, having regard to the constitution of the said order, as stated in petitioner's said former charge, and which, in order to avoid repetition, he begs may be taken as incorporated with this discharge, so far as the same relates to the said bequest." An affidavit has been made by Timothy Molony, Esq., Justice of the Peace, which states that the Roman Catholic church of Pope's Quay, in the city of Cork, to which the Rev. P. T. Conway is attached, is very largely frequented by the Catholics of Cork, and is one of the ordinary and principal places of Roman Catholic worship in said city. I am of opinion that the bequest to the Rev. P. T. Conway was invalid, as contrary to the policy of the 10th George IV., c. 7. The church belongs to the Order of Dominican Monks, bound together by monastic vows, and Rev. P. T. Conway is one of the members of the order, and the trust is for the redemption of the rent of their church. The fact that the Roman Catholic inhabitants may be permitted to attend the church cannot vary the question. I am also of opinion, for the reasons I have stated, in reference to the appeal of the Rev. R. White and the Rev. B. T. Russell, that charitable bequests contrary to the policy of the statute law or the common law should in general be carried out *cy pres*. The question of difficulty in the case of the bequest to the Rev. Mr. Conway is whether the principle of the Wheatley Church case, and the case of Carbery *v.* Cox, governs the bequest. I entertain doubt as to the Wheatley Church case, but it has been recognised by Lord Chancellor Blackburne in Carbery *v.* Cox, and by the Lord Chancellor in Daly *v.* the Attorney-General.[109] I do not see any sound distinction between the bequests of Carbery *v.* Cox of an

---

[109] The Master of the Rolls read the observations of the Lord Chancellor, in Daly *v.* the Attorney-General, 11th *Irish Chancery Reports*, 45-46, in relation to the Wheatley Church case, and the decision of Lord Chancellor Blackburne in Carbery *v.* Cox.

annuity to the monks of Mount Mellory, to be appropriated for the improvement of the chapel of Mellory, and the bequests to Mr. Conway which was in trust for the redemption of the rent of the chapel in Cork of the monks of Saint Dominic. I am bound by those decisions, and so far as the bequest to the Rev. Mr. Conway is concerned, I shall therefore declare that the bequest to Mr. Conway is void, and that it cannot be carried out *cy pres*. The Master's order will, therefore, be affirmed as to the bequest to the Rev. Mr. Conway, but will be varied as to the bequest to the Rev. Mr. White and the Rev. Mr. Russell. I myself entertain an opinion that the *cy pres* doctrine in charity cases is contrary to common sense, and have never been able to understand why the Court of Chancery is to make a will for a person which he did not himself make. This appears to have been Sir W. Grant's opinion according to his judgment in the case of Cary *v.* Abbot. The injustice was flagrant during the existence of the penal laws, when a bequest for the maintenance of Roman Catholic priests might be applied to the maintenance of clergymen of the Established Church. This was what judges in former days called *cy pres*, and the principle was very justly commented upon by Mr. Scully, in his well-known work on the penal laws. At present there is little, if any, injustice in the application of the principle of *cy pres*, because in this case, for example, the bequest to the Rev. Mr. White and the Rev. Mr. Russell might, on the reasonable application of the *cy pres* doctrine, be applied to the maintenance and education of two secular priests.

THE RELIGIOUS ORDERS—THE PENAL LAWS.

Five months after the adverse judgment passed on the Dominicans by the Master of the Rolls, an article, which I here give, appeared in the *Dublin Evening Post*. It relates to a public meeting which was to be held in the Chamber of Commerce of Cork by the leading citizens.

We perceive by our contemporary, the *Examiner*, that the citizens of Cork are to hold a public meeting, pursuant to requisition, under the presidency of the Mayor, to protest against the continuance of the penal law upon which the decision of all the Chancery tribunals, ending with the Court of Appeal, was founded in the case of Simms *v.* Quinlan. There is nothing more repulsively characteristic of the still vigorous spirit of English intolerance than the grafting of penalties, full of its worst instincts, upon measures even of benefit and relief, as in the case of Emancipation. Against the application of those penalties, or any apparent submission or indifference to the policy which has dictated them, it is the duty of Catholics not only to protest but to resist. In the case of Simms *v.* Quinlan, the operation of the penal clauses of the Emancipation Act affecting religious orders comes home to the door of the southern capital in a more especial manner, because it defeats the bounty of a Cork testator to a Cork community of the illustrious Order against which it has been enforced, and actually plunders, in the name of the law, a public institution which the people of Cork have endowed for their own spiritual service. Cork assembles to discharge its own immediate duty, and take the place of honour corresponding with the place of injury; but the citizens of Cork should not be left without the zealous support and encouragement of their countrymen all over Ireland; for, although the smart of this legislative iniquity by which the Fathers of St. Mary's have been divested of their property—

or rather of the property which they adminitser for the public—is local just at present, the iniquity itself is universal, and should meet with universal protest and resistance.

The Penal Laws *versus* the Dominican Fathers.

A numerously attended meeting, called on a requisition to the Mayor, signed by most of our leading citizens, was held on April 25th, 1865, at one o'clock in the Chamber of Commerce, for the purpose of entering a formal protest against the continuance of the old penal law on which the Chancellor's decision, depriving the Dominican Fathers of a bequest of £500 made to the Prior of St. Mary's for abating the rent of the church, was based.

Amongst those present were—The Mayor, N. D. Murphy, M.P.; John Francis Maguire, M.P.; D. Leahy Arthur, J.P., D.L.; Martin Hayes, William McNamara, J. N. Murphy, Timothy Mahony, J.P.; the Rev. J. J. Canon Murphy, William Hayes, Francis Lyons, T.C.; Maurice Murray, W. Galgey, Michael Sullivan, C. Cremen, John J. O'Connor, T.C.; Frederick Lyons, Edward McNamara, N. J. Murphy, T. Scannell, T.C.; Daniel Mulcahy, Bartholomew Daly, Robert Lambkin, James Dwyer, T.C.; D. Sheehan, Daniel Donegan, J.P., ald.; Nicholas Murphy, John Madden, Dr. Denis C. O'Connor, Daniel Finn, T.C.; Sir W. Hackett, Thomas Hayes, M. Barry, professor Q.C.C.; Daniel O'Sullivan, ex-high sheriff; J. W. Clery, J.P.; William J. Murphy, James J. O'Brien, D. McCarthy Mahony, C. Moynihan, John Hegarty, Patrick Hegarty, T.C.; William Hegarty, ALD.; Daniel F. Leahy, J.P.; John Sullivan, John A. Hanrahan, solicitor; Alexander McCarthy, J.P.; Daniel McSwiney, Mark O'Brien, James McSwiney, William McSwiney, John George MacCarthy, solicitor; Matthew O'Regan, Thomas Bresnan, John Hanrahan, W. O'Connell, David A. Nagle, Corns. Ahearne, R. Sutton, jun.; M. J. Collins, T.C.; Denis O'Flynn, S. O'Hea Cussen, Denis Hickie, T.C.; J. Slattery, Jas. O'Connor, T. McAuliffe, Anthony Murray, Dr. O'Flynn, Patrick Farrell, William Scannell, Ed. O'Regan, A. McCarthy, town clerk; Timothy Flynn, P. O'Sullivan, T.C.; John Hurley, Alderman Keller, Alexander Nichols, T. Barrett, T.C.; Edmund Burke, D.L.;

Barry J. Sheehan, T.C.; Peter Pennington, David O'Meara, Dr. Bullen, jun.; Andrew Fitzgerald, Thomas Waters. J. O'Callaghan, Michael Carey, etc.

On the motion of Mr. Maurice Murray, seconded by Mr. Patrick Hegarty, the chair was taken amidst applause by the Mayor.

Messrs. E. McNamara, N. Murphy, F. Lyons, and T. Bresnan were appointed secretaries.

The Mayor said he had convened this meeting to-day on a requisition signed by a very numerous and influential body, and in taking the chair he may say that he most heartily concurred in the objects for which this meeting was assembled. He held that every man is equal, and that every man, no matter what his religious denomination may be, is entitled to whatever the law of the land gave him as well as he was, but he demanded for himself and his co-religionists that they also should be allowed equal rights to whatever the law of the land gave them. It is quite true that in past times the Catholics have laboured under many serious disabilities; thanks to the Catholic Emancipation Act many of these disabilities have been removed, but a few still remain in the statute book which ought to be at once removed from it. He was not going to say anything about the disabilities under which they formerly laboured. With the past they had nothing to do. They could only look to the present. He was sure that in this matter there could be but one opinion. He was sure that if they were to take the opinion of all the citizens of Cork on the matter, irrespective of difference of religion, that, save some few fanatics, they would all agree in saying that this penal law, for such it was, should no longer degrade the statute book. They met there to ask Parliament for the relief of a most praiseworthy and noble community from a grievous and unjust statute. They were there to ask the Government to remove from the statute book clauses which were intended to satisfy a bigoted party, and which should certainly not in the middle of the enlightened nineteenth century any longer remain part of the laws of Great Britain.

Mr. N. D. Murphy proposed the first resolution. He said—
Mr. Mayor and gentlemen, the duty has devolved on me of proposing the first resolution. I wish most sincerely that, occupying the public position I now do, I had made it a duty of my earlier life to prepare myself for doing well and properly what I am now called on to do, namely, to propose an important resolution at a great public meeting. However that may be, I must take to myself that I am sincere, most sincere in wishing well to the object for which this meeting was called together, and I ask you, gentlemen, that with whatever want of ability I may speak to the resolution, that you will at any rate give me credit for perfect sincerity. I do not know, sir, that it will be necessary for me, or, indeed, for any person whose duty it will be to address you to-day, to urge on this meeting the adoption of this resolution by any very formidable array of arguments or great collection of facts. We are met here to-day because a great wrong has been done to a most useful religious community in this city. That honoured and respectable community has been put by the laws of this country into such a position that they are no longer entitled to receive whatever sums any citizen of Cork may in the free exercise of their judgment think proper to give them. But independently altogether of this, the most important part of the whole is that the Act of Catholic Emancipation, the Act which its preamble stated itself to be an Act to relieve the Catholic subjects of her Majesty—this act of relief actually contained a clause which placed upon the statute book of the kingdom a penal statute against the priesthood, which had actually never before existed at all, even in the worst days of the Penal Laws This clause was inserted by the statesman who passed the Emancipation Act as a kind of sop—a kind of tub to a whale—in order to satisfy the intolerance of those who would but for the introduction of this and similar clauses have opposed and perhaps succeeded in throwing out the bill. I venture to say that very few of the gentlemen assembled here to-day, very few of the people of this country, are aware that until the passing of the Emancipation Act this clause never existed. I say, sir,

that there is no reason whatever why this clause should not at once be abolished—no sound reason whatever that it should for a single session darken the pages of the statute book. As I have said that clause and the others were not opposed, in order not to imperil the bill, but they were introduced by the ministry and consented to by the Catholics on the full understanding that they were to remain a dead letter. Those clauses are not then at all, properly speaking, parts of the act of relief passed at the time. They were merely introduced to satisfy a feeling now happily passed away, and then immediate repeal was called for. The clause does not stand alone. I shall just read another clause, which enacts that if "any Jesuit or member of any such religious order shall after the passing of this Act come into the realm he shall be deemed guilty of a misdemeanour, and shall he banished from the kingdom for the term of his natural life." Was this an enactment which ought to be allowed on the statute book? I say most decidedly it should not. There were comments made on this clause at the time, and it was said that Catholic countries also banished the Jesuits, and why should not England do the same thing. Now it would be all very well if the Catholic religion was on the same conditions in the countries where this had been done, as in England, but such was not the case. In these countries the Catholic religion was the religion of the State, the episcopal appointments were recognised, and there may be some show of reason for the claims made by the State to a right to banish the Jesuits; but in England, where Catholicity was merely tolerated, it was quite plain no such right could exist. The speaker then read an extract from a speech delivered during the debate on the Catholic question by Mr. Labouchere, and which set forth that as long as any persons behave themselves properly their religious opinions ought not be interfered with. He then continued to say—Such are the words of one of the ablest statesmen of the day, and I do not think it necessary to detain you any longer by any further remarks. I shall merely point out another matter, which is much of a similar nature with these objectionable

clauses. Another clause introduced into the Emancipation Act,
in order to soothe the prejudices of those who imagined that the
country would be seriously injured by the passing of the Act, was
a clause which enacted that your worship, or any other Catholic
mayor, should not carry into a place of worship the insignia of
your office. I really think one of those clauses is just as ridiculous
as the other. I do not know, sir, whether it is quite correct to
introduce to this meeting any matter except the one which
we have actually come to determine, but I cannot help saying
that this matter is only part of a greater question which our
legislators will one day have to decide on, namely, the position
of the Established Church in Ireland. There is no doubt that
the very least that can be required by the people of Ireland,
composing, as they do, four-fifths of the population of the country,
is, at least, religious equality. I speak not of religious superiority,
although in justice and right reason the population of any country
is entitled to have as the religion of the State that in which
the majority of its people believe. That question I am not
about to enter on, but I repeat that to religious equality at least
the people of this country are entitled, and until the anomaly of
an Established Church, professing a religion different from the
majority of the people, is removed, the country can never either
be prosperous or contented. The right hon. gentleman concluded by referring to a speech delivered in 1864 by a man
who certainly was no warm adherent of the Roman Catholic
Church, Mr. Benjamin Disraeli, in which he recommends as the
only cure for the condition of Ireland, "perfect religious and
political equality." He proposed the following resolution:—

Resolved—"That the continuance of penal enactments against the
persons and property of some of the most eminent, most useful, and
most respected of the Catholic clergy of these kingdoms is a flagrant
abuse and injustice, and a disgrace to civilization."

Mr. D. F. Leahy seconded the resolution. He said that the
thanks of the Catholic community at large were due to the
Rev. Prior of St. Mary's for bringing this matter before the public.

Everyone knew well that no one was more retiring than the reverend gentleman; no man would be more sorry to have to enter a court of law, and for these very reasons the reverend gentleman deserved their most sincere thanks for contending in the manner he did against the attempts made to deprive his Order of the bequest left to them by a charitable fellow-citizen. Had not public attention been drawn to this matter by the courageous conduct of this reverend gentlemen, the disgraceful clause in question would have been allowed to remain unnoticed on the statute book.

The resolution was then passed unanimously.

Mr. Maguire, M.P., proposed the second resolution. He said—Mr. Mayor and gentlemen—Mr. Leahy has made a very pertinent, and, in my opinion, a most apposite remark. He has said that we, the Catholics of Cork, are deeply indebted to the Prior of St. Mary's for having formally brought this question under the notice of the Catholics of the empire. Now, it is not the first time that the Catholics of Cork and of Ireland have been indebted to the Dominican Order. If any Catholic, interested in the records of his church, will only look back to the history of the country for the last three hundred years, he will find that by no one branch of the great religious Orders, which have been the pride and glory of his church, have greater services been done to the Catholic faith and the followers of that faith than by that illustrious Order. At one time the Order of St. Dominic was great and powerful in Ireland. It had its seats of learning, possessed noble priories and convents, it enjoyed large revenues, and it had larger hearts to administer them for the service of religion and the benefit of God's poor. But when the hand of the spoiler was heavy upon them—when their sanctuaries were desecrated, when their roof trees were given to the torch, when they were scattered abroad and hunted through the land as felons—I ask did the Fathers of St. Dominic even then desert the country and desert their flocks? If we seek for an answer to this query we shall find it in contemporary history—that the more eagerly were they sought to be driven from the country the more earnestly did they

cling to the soil, and the more zealously did they strive to keep
alive the spirit of the old faith in the breast of a down-trodden
and persecuted race. Among the religious Orders of Ireland
there was no greater zeal manifested or more sublime heroism
displayed than by the noble followers of St. Dominic. We,
then, not only owe a debt of gratitude to the venerated Prior of
St. Mary's for his courage and determination in fighting a battle
of principle on behalf of the Catholics of this city, but we, in
common with our brethren throughout Ireland, owe a lasting
obligation to the Order itself for the priceless services which
it rendered to endangered faith in the worst hours of a
blighting persecution. Mr. Murphy referred in his admirable
address to that so-called measure of Catholic relief, the Emancipation Act, and he has said, which is historically true, that
Sir Robert Peel and the promoters of the measure were obliged
to propitiate the rampant spirit of intolerance which offered the
greatest obstacle to the passing of any measure of relief. It
is a most interesting thing for us Catholics of the present
day to look back to the history and incidents of the great
struggle, and we cannot do so without feeling a lively sense
of gratitude—not to the Dominican Fathers who bled upon
the scaffold or pined in the dungeon in defence of the faith,
but to the gallant, though humble, frieze-coated peasants of
Clare, who really broke the chains that had been forged in
blood and fire nearly three hundred years before. It is a
curious thing to consider the spirit in which the Emancipation
Act was proposed, and what were the feelings of those who were
its proposers. For instance, one of the statesmen who earnestly
advised the English Government of that day to propose and
carry a settlement of the Catholic claims, wrote an important
and confidential letter, which had a good deal to do with the
pushing on of the question, and which commenced in these
words—"I must begin by premising that I hold in abhorrence
the association, the agitators, the priests, and their religion."
That was the expression of the inner mind of one who was still
anxious that the Catholic claims should be adjusted, and that the

danger to which the existing state of things gave rise should be
put an end to. That was written by the Marquess of Anglesey,
then Lord Lieutenant of Ireland. It was by the awakened
energy of the Catholic people of Ireland, it was mainly by the
courage and self-devotion of the Catholic peasantry of Clare,
that Emancipation was forced from one of the most unwilling
Cabinets that ever attempted to deal with an unpalatable and
obnoxious question. Sir Robert Peel was always averse, and
on what he conceived to be great and even lofty principles of
Protestant statesmanship, to conceding anything to the Catholic
cause. The Duke of Wellington was just as averse. The great
mass of the English people were in reality opposed to a com-
prehensive settlement. And thus it was to the Catholic people
of Ireland, led well and wisely by O'Connell, that the great
boon of Emancipation was wrested from King, from Cabinet,
from Church, and from Parliament. It was with the utmost
difficulty that Sir Robert Peel, the Duke of Wellington, and
Lord Lyndhurst could obtain the sanction of the King to make
even the slightest allusion to a possible settlement of the
Catholic claims in the Royal Speech. And after Sir Robert
Peel, as the spokesman of the Cabinet and the leader of the
House of Commons, had given notice that he would, on the
5th of March, bring the motion referred to in the Speech before
the House, he was informed that the King had withdrawn his
consent to the proposal of any measure of relief. The Cabinet
was practically broken up, and it was only at the last hour—in
fact only a few hours before the motion was to be brought
forward, that the King consented to allow, as he said, his
ministers to " go on." At that time all Ireland was in a flame.
The Catholics were eager and determined to be free from the
last link of a galling slavery that had lasted for centuries, and
was illustrated by every description of persecution—confiscations,
plunder, cruelty, and degradation. There was, on the other
hand, a great amount of ultra-Protestant feeling that could not be
propitiated, and that imagined that all kinds of horrors were to
be the result of freedom to their Catholic brethren. I need not

describe the state of things in England ; but looking back to these times, and judging of them by the light of the memoir left by Sir Robert Peel, as well as by other records, it must be clear that the ministers of that day had a work of the greatest and most critical difficulty to undertake ; and the wonder is how, in spite of the opposition of the King, the Church, the powerful Protestant or anti-Catholic party, and the lukewarmness of the Cabinet, Emancipation was carried as soon as it was. But if it has done good, and conferred a boon on Catholics generally, it has inflicted a positive wrong on those who now appeal to us for sympathy and protection. Mr. Leahy has said that he never knew that such provisions existed as have now started up into vicious activity. Why, sir, you have the statement of Dr. Russell to the effect that, when the representatives of the religious Orders were sent over to London to watch their imperilled interests, not only did the advocates and real friends of Emancipation assure them that the clauses in question, which were passed to propitiate the enemies to all Catholic claims, would remain a dead letter, but that the same was asserted by the promoters of the Bill—by the ministers themselves. In fact it was distinctly understood that they were to remain inoperative, and would never be put in force. But now you have seen how this slumbering iniquity has sprung into life. If we, Catholic laymen, stand here this day as freemen, emancipated, the equals of our Protestant brethren, there is one class not free, one class not emancipated, who still retain, clanking round them, fetters of the chain forged for our Catholic forefathers three hundred years since. It is our duty to protest against the continued existence of these iniquitous clauses. I do not hold out the delusive hope that they will be at once repealed ; but this is no reason why we should tamely endure their existence. If a wrong be done you, it is not because you cannot obtain immediate redress that you are not to proclaim that it is, as in this case, a wrong, an insult, and a grievance. But we have assembled here to-day for something more than the mere entering of a protest against obnoxious clauses of the Act of

Emancipation; we have assembled for another purpose than to pay a merited compliment to one of the most meritorious and illustrious of the religious Orders of our country—we have met to free them from a pecuniary difficulty, we have met for the purpose of giving back to them what a Catholic on his dying bed imagined he had a perfect right to bequeath to them, but which an unjust law took from them. A respectable Catholic citizen made a bequest to the Prior of St. Mary's. For what purpose? To abate the rent of a church which belongs to every Catholic in the city. And if any purpose should have saved that bequest from the meshes of an iniquitous law, the purpose to which it was to be applied should have done so; but the Chancellor who administered the law administered it only according to its letter and spirit, and we Catholics say nothing against his interpretation of the law. The Dominican Fathers not only lost £500, but £200 besides. Our first obligation to those gentlemen is to repay them the £200 incurred in costs; our next is to restore to them the £500 of which the law, in our opinion, wrongfully deprived them. The Catholics of Cork are ready and willing to pay the entire £700, and they ought to do so as the most solemn and emphatic protest against a law which, passed under false pretences, is a disgrace to the statute book of a country calling itself free. The Dominican Fathers incurred these heavy costs in a contest of principle, and we are indebted to them for their courage and determination. After one or two other observations Mr. Maguire read the resolution, which is as follows:—

Resolved—" That the recent decision against the venerated Prior of St. Mary's, showing that these penal enactments can still be enforced, and depriving a public church of the endowment which a fellow-citizen bequeathed to it, calls for a prompt and emphatic protest from the citizens of Cork,"

A "prompt" protest, gentlemen, we have given; but the "emphatic" protest remains to be recorded—recorded in the face of our fellow-citizens, in the face of our country, and in the face of the Imperial Parliament; and that emphatic protest will be to lodge in the bank, to the credit of the Prior of St. Mary's, the sum of £500, of which an iniquitous law deprived him, and the £200 which he incurred in a spirit alike of devotion to religion and liberty, for which devotion we now offer him our earnest thanks. I beg, sir, to propose the resolution.

Mr. D. O'Sullivan seconded the resolution, and in doing so trusted that the Roman Catholics of Ireland would, by a unanimous effort, procure from the House of Commons the repeal of the clause under which an act of such injustice had been done.

The resolution was passed unanimously.

Mr. J. N. Murphy proposed the next resolution, and said that there was very little necessity for his adding anything to the valuable statements which were made by Mr. Maguire in the course of his eloquent address. He would commence by saying that all they asked for was that which he was sure every one of his fellow-citizens, whatever might be his religion, would be ready to concede to them, namely, perfect equality, which he thought was a right that ought to be enjoyed by every citizen of this empire living peaceably and paying taxes. As to his Protestant fellow-citizens, he was happy to say that they would all admit the justice of this demand. The condition of Ireland had lately occupied a great deal of attention in the House of Commons and elsewhere in England, and there had been letters in the *Times* and in the other leading papers, in which it was stated that Ireland had nothing whatever to complain of. Now, the object for which they were obliged to meet to-day was a fact that showed that the statement that Ireland had nothing to complain of was erroneous. The Act, some of the clauses of which they now sought to have repealed, was the Emancipation Act—the 10th George IV. On referring to that Act he found some very extraordinary clauses in it. In the 7th clause it was provided that all Jesuits and members of other religious Orders in Ireland should, within one month after the passing of the Act, send in their names to the Clerk of the Peace, and that if they did not do so they should be liable to a penalty of

£50 a month for whatever time they should fail to comply with the Act. There was another clause which provided that if any Jesuits or members of other religious Orders came into Ireland after the passing of the Act they should be obliged to quit the country within thirty days for the remainder of their lives, and that if they did not do so they should be taken, tried, and banished for the term of their lives. Immediately before the Emancipation Act was passed an influential deputation went from the city of Cork and waited on the Prime Minister (the Duke of Wellington) in London. The Right Rev. Dr. Leahy, the bishop of Dromore, who was a member of that deputation, told him (Mr. Murphy) that the Duke, when spoken to about these clauses, said that it was necessary to insert them to satisfy the prejudices of persons whose opposition would otherwise cause the entire rejection of the Act, but that those clauses would be null, and that they were always intended to remain so. They all knew the circumstances under which the bequest in question was left. The late Mr. Simms left a bequest to the Fathers of St. Mary's, and the object for which the bequest was left was to decrease the rent of the chapel. The intention was a perfectly just one, and yet the law said that that intention was not to be carried out. It was promised, as he had said, by the Duke of Wellington and by all the members of the Cabinet that the clauses to which he had referred would not be carrried out, and yet here they found a gentleman who in order to invalidate the bequest, asked to have those clauses enforced. Now, Mr. Simms left the bequest to those pious and worthy clergymen, the Dominican Fathers of this city, for a laudable purpose, and yet under those clauses they were deprived of it. He did not mean to say that the Lord Chancellor did not decide properly, for he was sure that the Chancellor only did what he was bound to do, but the law stepped in and said that every bequest made to those pious gentlemen was invalid. If a member of the Jewish synagogue in Dublin left, in order to pay the rent of the synagogue, a sum of money to the clergyman conducting it the law could not interfere. He would not for a moment say that the Jews or any other body ought not to have perfect freedom, or that they should be in any way interfered with. He would say that all men should enjoy perfect equality, religious and political, but he would ask were three-fourths of the population of Ireland—were some four and a-half millions of people—not to enjoy the same privileges as three hundred and twenty-two Jews. Were not the Roman Catholics of Ireland to be placed on an equal footing as regarded religious and political freedom with these people? Were they not to be in the same position, especially when the proportion in point of number was fourteen thousand to one? He could not help asking was it just that Jews, who did not believe in the redemption of mankind by our Saviour, should be entitled to a right which was refused to the religion of a great people—the religion which, in common with all other Christian creeds, had as its fundamental principle the redemption of mankind by our Lord. He believed that the most important part of the meeting was the petition that it was intended to present to Parliament on this question. That petition being presented would be quickly followed by a motion, and when attention was drawn to the matter he ventured to assert that nine out of ten of the English members would support that motion. It would obtain the support of a party in England which was now a power in the State, and which in future times would be a greater power still—he meant the great Manchester party. It was to that party they had to look for the removal of the disabilities which still pressed on the Catholics of Ireland. He was sure that when their attention was pointed to the matter their full assistance would be granted, and that the clauses would be repealed. The question of the Protestant ascendancy, which now occupied so much attention, would receive the full consideration of the Manchester party, and to that party the Roman Catholics of Ireland and of England should look for being placed in a position of religious and political equality with their fellow-citizens. He felt that there was scarcely any necessity for him to make reference to the services of the Dominican Order in this country in past times. Many of the priests of that Order suffered death when the penal laws were in full force in the cause of religion and charity. During those fearful times, when the penal laws were at their height, it was the law of the land that if any Jesuit or any member of a religious order was found in this country he should be hanged and quartered. They would find it stated in the *Hibernia Dominicana* that in those times numbers of the pious and zealous members of the Order suffered the last punishment of the law for nothing but for having preached the Gospel. The pious fathers of the Order now in this city had imitated the example of their predecesssors, and the citizens were bound to do everything in their power to support them. To do so the present meeting was called, and he believed that the case of Simms *versus* the Dominican Fathers, although it caused those gentlemen a good deal of present annoyance, would be in the end the means of removing from the statute book the last penal enactment against the Catholics of this country. Mr. Murphy then concluded by moving the following resolution :—

Resolved—" That however deeply we might feel the wrong and insult if we were ourselves thus treated by law as only felons and outlaws are treated, we feel far more deeply indignant that this wrong and insult should be inflicted on peaceful and holy clergymen, whose lives are ceaselessly devoted to works of charity and piety, against whom not one word of reproach has ever been said or written, and who are endeared to the whole Catholic community by priceless services rendered and the noblest example afforded."

Mr. McCarthy said—Mr. Mayor and gentlemen, I beg to second the resolution so ably proposed by Mr. Murphy. It is not necessary that I should occupy your time with many comments. Indeed it is almost imposible to do so. O'Connell himself used to say, " Give me a difficult and doubtful case and I will argue about it for ten days if you like. Give me a perfectly clear case and I will find it difficult to argue about it for ten minutes." Now this is just one of those perfectly clear cases which it is alike almost unnecessary and almost impossible to argue about. The laws of the country find certain clergymen, our fellow-citizens, and it says to them, without why or wherefore—you are outlaws! It is true you are associated only for purposes of charity and piety—to practise those sacred counsels which the Divine author of Christianity taught from the Sacred Mount—we care not, you are outlaws! It is true that your lives are so absolutely blameless that not even calumny itself has a reproach to whisper. We care not— you are outlaws! It is true that your lives are entirely blameless, but are spent in good works, and are endeared by priceless services rendered to every Catholic family in the community. We care not—you are outlaws! You're outlaws—we will confiscate the property which is as clearly yours as the property of any man here is his—nay, we have power to attack your persons, to say to you, you must not breathe your native air, or if you do we will give you a felon's shame and a felon's doom! Now, is there any man in this room, is there any man in this community, who has one single word to say in defence of such a law as this? It is true that as to personal attacks the fathers are safe. There are two reasons for this. One reason is that no one would wish to enforce them, another, a plainer and a simpler reason, is, that they dared not be enforced. The Ministry that would attempt to enforce them would be attacked by all classes and parties and swept out of office in a week. Even as regards their property, it also is generally safe, and this is also for two reasons. One reason is, that by a simple arrangement the law may be evaded. Another and clearer reason is, that most men would rather sweep the streets or beg from door to door than to make use of a penal law to deprive venerable clergymen of what is as certainly and honestly theirs as my coat is mine. And who are they whom the law thus wrongs and insults? We have many old civic families in Cork, but none older, none more respected, than the family of St. Dominic. For six hundred years and more their fathers have served our fathers. In olden times the abbey of St. Mary's was the pride of Cork. It sent its doctors to the great councils of the Church. It sent prelates to rule not only Cork and Cloyne and Cashel, but Cologne and Mayence and Besançon. It offered its munificent hospitalities to native princes; and when a Lord Lieutenant came to Cork it was at St. Mary's of the Isle he lodged. In the dark penal times they were ever true to us. A father of the convent, rather than tarnish by one stain the white robe of St. Dominic, submitted to be burned alive on the Rock of Cashel—a flaming beacon of the injustice of the time, and of the indomitable heroism that conquered the injustice. In after days at the old friary in Friary Lane—in the more recent friary in Dominic Street—they brought the learning and talents that had won rare honours in foreign universities to minister to the wants of Cork. And in latter times who will say that they have not been worthy of their Order and their predecessors? Who does not feel any insult or injury to them as an injury and insult to himself? But the matter may be put on even broader grounds. We object to injustice because it is unjust. And if it so happened to-morrow that any body of Protestant clergymen, being men of blameless lives and spotless character, were banned by the law as the Dominican Fathers are banned, we would assemble then, as we have assembled to-day, to protest against the injustice with our persons, with our voices, with our purses, and with our hearts. Mr. McCarthy concluded by seconding the resolution.

Mr. J. W. Clery proposed the next resolution, which was as follows :—

Resolved—"That the Mayor, the secretaries, and the proposers and seconders of resolutions be constituted a committee to prepare a petition to Parliament for remedying this abuse, which petition shall be signed by the Mayor as chairman of this meeting, and be entrusted for presentation to the members for the city, aided by Mr. Maguire, M.P."

Dr. O'Connor seconded the resolution. He said that he had heard with great pleasure the many speeches delivered, and observed that now, as ever, Corkmen were directed by the dictates of prudence and good sense. They were determined to obtain, by means strictly constitutional, the repeal of a very obnoxious clause, which in common with a few others disfigured a most useful Act. At the same time he thought that the Government were not to blame for the long continuance of these clauses on the statute books. They had been there now for nearly forty years, and yet the Government had never been asked to repeal them. It was then the Catholics of Ireland who were to blame.

Mr. D. O'Flynn moved as an amendment that the members named in the resolution be requested to draw up a substantial resolution to bring before the House.

There being no seconder to the amendment the original resolution was passed unanimously.

The Mayor was then moved from the chair, Mr. Maguire moved thereto, and a vote of thanks passed to his worship for his dignified conduct in the chair.

Mr. W. Hegarty moved the following resolution :—

Resolved—" That, as the best practical protest against the injustice which the law has inflicted on the Fathers of St. Mary's Church, a subscription list be now opened to make up the sum of £500, of which the law has unjustly deprived them, together with the expenses incurred, and that the committee make arrangements for carrying out the collections."

He said that there were a few facts connected with the present church and priory of St. Mary's which may not prove uninteresting to the meeting. The old church was, as many of them knew, a very small, uncomfortable structure, built in a narrow little street in the back part of the city. The Rev. Mr. Russell succeeded, by great exertions, in erecting in place of the old church the noble building which was now an ornament to the city and a memorial to the pious munificence of the Catholics of Cork. The clergymen of St. Mary's had, however, to pay for this church a very heavy ground rent. In order to lessen or remove this heavy rent a worthy citizen of Cork left of his own free will a large sum of money. Now the law intervened and it said to those pious clergymen, those men who did more to prevent vice from being prevalent in Cork than all the officers of the law—it said to those men, " You cannot receive this bequest." Such a law should never have existed, but as it did exist its repeal was imperatively called for. The Rev. Mr. Russell, not satisfied with having built a noble church, also erected a handsome priory, and when erecting the priory he sent for him (Mr. Hegarty), who was then chairman of the building committee, and said to him that there was a quantity of stone in the Corporation yard which he wanted for the building, and for which he offered to give £70. On mentioning the matter to Mr. A. Deane, who was on the committee, that gentleman said to give them to Father Russell for £2 10s., and the elder Mr. Jameson said, in reply to a remark of his, that Father Russell deserved the stone twenty times better than did the Protestant clergyman who got the stones of the old Exchange to build the tower of St. Fin Barr's. This showed the spirit with which the Protestants of Cork regarded the Dominican brethren. The church of St. Mary's and the priory were both built, and into them were built many of the stones of the convent of St. Mary's of the Isle, destroyed by the hand of the spoiler centuries ago.

The resolution was seconded by Mr. T. Hayes, and passed unanimously.

A subscription list was then opened, and a large sum collected, after which the proceedings terminated.

Our Lady of Youghal—"St. Mary of Graces."

(Page 118.)

The Dominican historians, John O'Heyn[110] and Dr. Burke, the Bishop of Ossory, otherwise Thomas de Burgo,[111] tell us of the existence of the miraculous statue of the Blessed Virgin in the convent of Youghal. Dr. Burke makes mention of it in the following words:—

"A most pious image of the ever Blessed Mother of God was formerly preserved in the sacred precincts of this convent, to which the faithful used to have recourse from all parts of Ireland, *voti causa*, that is, on account of a vow which they had made to do so. In the acts of the Most General Chapter, held in Rome, 1644, under the fifty-sixth Master-General of the Order, Thomas Turco, of Cremona, a decree is extant applying all the alms offered in honour of the most pious image of the Blessed Virgin of Youghal to the convent of that town, and ordering the Provincial not to dispose of them otherwise."

About one hundred years before the time of Dr. Burke, Boullaye le Gouz, who was known by his contemporaries under the title of the "Catholic Traveller," on account of having visited most, if not all, the countries of the world, gives us, in a work which he published in 1653, descriptive of his travels,

[110] *Epilogus Chronologicus.*
[111] *Hibernia Dominicana*, pp. 239, 272, 273.

THE DOMINICANS. 187

a very interesting account of the image of "the Virgin of God," as he expresses it, which had been venerated in the Dominican church of Youghal some years before his arrival in that town. The account is full of quaint-

SIEUR BOULLAYE LE GOUZ.

ness and expressions of simple piety. These are his words:—

"In the convent of St. Dominic was the image of the Virgin of God, which had been formerly the object of the greatest devotion in Ireland. It arrived there (Youghal) in a miraculous manner. The tide brought a piece of wood to the river's bank adjoining the town, and a number of fishermen wished to take it away, the wood being rare in this place, but they could not remove it. They harnessed ten horses for the purpose, without any effect. On its return the tide carried it towards the Dominican Convent, when two religious put it on their shoulders and placed it in the courtyard of the convent. The Father Superior during the night had a vision informing him that the image of our Lady, the Virgin of great power, was in this wood, and accordingly it was found in it. This is what is said about it by the Catholics, who up to the present have the greatest devotion towards it; but the Dominicans, having been persecuted by the English settlers, have carried it elsewhere."[112]

We learn from Sir John Pope Hennessy, the late Governor of the Mauritius, in his book entitled *Sir Walter Raleigh in Ireland*[113]—

"That in 1586 the Dominican Friary, which had been built in Youghal by Thomas Fitzmaurice Fitzgerald in 1268, was granted to Raleigh. During his mayoralty of Youghal in 1587 he ordered or allowed the destruction of this fine building, the massive piers and broken arches of which still remain. Raleigh's agents in the demolition, according to a book[114] published in 1620, were unfortunate. 'An Englishman breaking down the monastrie of S. Dominique's in Youghall fell dead from the toppe of the church, all his limmes being broken, A.D. 1587. Also three soldiers who did caste downe and burne the holy roode of that monastrie died within one seanight after they had done it.'"

[112] *Les Voyages et Observations du Sieur Boullaye le Gouz*, p. 454.
[113] Page 63.
[114] *Theatre of Catholique and Protestant Religion*, p. 124, quoted by the Rev. S. Hayman in his book on Youghal.

Sir John Pope Hennessy also says in his work on Raleigh[115]—

"The miraculous image of the Virgin, which made the monastery famous throughout Europe, was saved from Raleigh and his soldiers by the daughter of one of the Geraldines whom he had pursued."

"From Raleigh's time to this," the same writer remarks, "there has been a perpetual succession of Dominican custodians of the ruined abbey and the sacred image, the Rev. B. Russell, of Cork, being the present holder of that office (1883)."

It is interesting to know that Father Russell was historiographer of the *Hibernia Dominicana* from 1832 till the time of his death, 1890.

In the *History of Cork* by the Rev. C. B. Gibson, M.R.I.A., London, 1861 (p. 369) the following observations relative to this cherished image, as well as to that of S. Dominic, are made:—

"The Dominican Friars were at one time possessed of two highly-prized relics—the image of S. Dominic and of the Blessed Virgin Mary. Matthew Cheyne, the Protestant Bishop of Cork, laid violent hands on the image of S. Dominic in 1578, and had it publicly burnt at the High Cross, to the great grief of the Irish of that place. The miraculous image of the Blessed Virgin is a carving in ivory, about three inches long, and a good deal worn and discoloured by time; it is in the custody of the friars, preserved in a silver case."

The Rev. Samuel Hayman, B.A., in his *Notes and Records of the Ancient Religious Foundations of Youghal*, 1855 (p. 47), refers to this statue in the following manner:—

"The image of the Madonna and Child, for which this friary

[115] Page 64.

was famous, is of Italian workmanship of the fifteenth century. It is of carved ivory, about three inches high. Lady Honor Fitzgerald, of the Geraldine family, presented the Dominicans of Youghal with a silver gilt shrine[116] for the image when in their possession."

In a note at the foot of the same page he says:—

"This shrine and image (of Youghal) are beautifully illustrated in *The Ulster Journal of Archæology*, April, 1854."

The illustrations are in connection with a most interesting article[117] concerning the image by the same writer, whom we have just quoted. It concludes with the following words:—

"The writer's obligations are due to his gifted friend, Thomas Crofton Croker, F.S.A., for much kind assistance in procuring the illustrations of the shrine. He would offer his respectful thanks to Mrs. Collins, daughter of the 'Roscoe' of Cork, the late James Roche. To this lady's pencil the open front view of the shrine is to be attributed. He begs to acknowledge also the kindness of the Rev. Mr. Russell, Superior O.S.D., Dublin, and of the Rev. Mr. Carbery, of St. Mary's Priory, Cork, through whose permission the other drawings have been made. The whole are now, for the first time, given to the public."

In order not to pass over anything which would tend to throw light on this cherished relic and its surroundings, I shall here, in conclusion, give an interesting extract from the *Historical and Descriptive Notices of the City of Cork*, published in 1849, by John Windele.

[116] See illustration, page 119.

[117] This is one of two papers which are headed, "Relics of Antiquities at Youghal, County Cork," by the Rev. Samuel Hayman, B.A. The other paper concerns "An Ancient Pectoral Cross found at Youghal in 1814."

Having dilated on the beauties of the then new church of St. Mary's, Pope's Quay, and also having given an account of "St. Mary's of the Isle," of some of its inmates, and its varying fortunes, he continues to say, at page 75 :—

"After the year 1690 the work of eradicating was effectually executed, and for the next sixty or seventy years the brethren diminished in numbers, and cowering under the heaviness of persecution concealed themselves in the by-parts of the city. The last place of their sojourn, previously to their occupying their present convent on the hill of Shandon, was in Friary Lane, an obscure and narrow passage leading off from Shandon Street, where they congregated in concealment until the relaxation of the penal code. Of their splendid priory on the island not a vestige [118] now remains. The site was until lately occupied by a distillery (St. Dominic's distillery) and a brewery. Strange transformation! The present convent is quite in keeping with the altered fortunes of the fraternity. It is a plain and undistinguished building. Amongst its relics is the miraculous image of the blessed Virgin Mary, formerly belonging to the Dominican Convent at Youghal, and whereof mention is made in the acts of the General Chapter held in Rome in 1644."

He then describes the image, and appears to agree with Mr. Crofton Croker as to the identity of "Onoria," the donor of the silver case in 1617, with the daughter of Sir James Desmond, who was killed in 1597.

He closes his remarks about Dominick Street Friary by saying :—

"As conventual records must be kept in every Dominican community, according to one of the constitutions of the Order (Rome, 1608), Bourke had great facilities in the compilation of

[118] See note, page 2.

his work,(119) as historiographer. That office is now held by the Rev. Bartholomew Russell, of St. Mary's, Cork, a gentleman fully qualified, by his talents and industry, to fulfil its interesting duties. In that capacity he now holds several of the MS. chronicles and documents formerly held by Bishop Bourke."

(119) *Hibernia Dominicana.*

THE END.

Index.

A.

Achilli, Apostate, 48
Address to Dr. Leahy, o.p , 56
Address to Thomas Bresnan, 98
Appeal, Public, for Funds, 106
ARCHITECTS—
  Atkins, William, 23
  Deane, Kearns, Architect of St. Mary's Church, Cork, alluded to,* 25
  Goldie, Mr., 41, 69, 123
  Hurley, John, 63
  Hynes, Mr., 97
ARCHITECTURE—
  Gothic Style, 31, 114
  Italian Rennaisance, 76
  Romanesque, 31
Archives of the Franciscan Fathers, Cork, 128
Australia, 62
Austria, 96
ARTISTS, SCULPTORS—
  Brennan, Mr., 100
  Cahill, Mr., 63
  Hogan, Mr., 40, 63
AUTHORS—
  Alemand, 131
  Archdall, 4
  Boullave le Gouz, 118, 121, 186, 187
  Burke, Rev. T., o.p., 6
  Campbell, 47
  Crofton Croker, 121, 122, 190, 191
  Dante, *title page*

Authors, *contd.*—
  De Burgo, o.p., 130
  Downing, Ellen, 21
  Echard, o.p., 131
  Gibson, Rev. C. B., ix., 3, 8, 122, 189
  Harris, 131
  Hayman, Rev. Samuel, 116, 117, 122, 188, 189, 190
  Longfellow, *title page*
  McCarthy, Denis Florence, 74
  Madden, R. R., 65, 67
  Moore, Thomas, 47
  O'Heyne, o.p., 14, 131
  Proctor, Adelaide A, 37, 52, 113
  Roche James, 46, 121
  Russell, Father, o.p., x, 47
  Smith Charles, 113, 131, 132
  Wadding o.s.f., 128
  Ware, 127, 131

B.

Barry, Standish, of Leamlara, 47
Benefactors, 144
Bequests Bill, Charitable, 19
BISHOPS and other Dignitaries of the Dominican Order—
  Blond, John le, 3
  Burgo, Dominic de, 9
  Carbery, James Joseph, 77, 78, 99
  Corcagiensis, Joannes, 4
  Flood, Patrick Vincent, 69, 89, 90, 91
  French, Dr., 22
  Gonin, Dr., 88

* The following inscription may be seen on a marble slab in the porch leading to the south aisle of St. Mary's, Pope's Quay :—

" The Dominican Community of Cork inscribe this stone in testimony of their gratitude to Kearns Deane, Esq., Architect, who with unexampled generosity and public spirit designed this building and directed the progress of its erection. 1832."

INDEX.

Bishops and other Dignitaries of the Dominican Order, *contd.*—
Griffiths, Dr., 46
Hyland, Thomas Raymond, 86, 87
Hynes, John, 22, 37, 38, 39, 40
Leahy John Pius, 55, 56, 60, 66, 92, 95, 96, 98, 99
McKelly, David, 2
O'Callaghan, Thomas Alphonsus, *dedication*, 60, 83, 84, 85, 86, 89, 92, 96, 102
O'Carroll, William Dominic, 64
O'Hurley, James, 8, 123
Oliffe, Dr., 47
O'Sullivan, Allan, 2, 3
Salua, Monsignor, 84
Slane, Philip de, 3
Wall, Peter, 7
Zigliara, Cardinal, 100
Other Bishops and Ecclesiastical Dignitaries—
Blake, Dr., 94
Browne, Dr. 101
Burgess, Dr., 80
Butler, Dr., s.J., 89
Colossus, Archbishop of, 39
Crolly, Dr., 22
Crotty, Dr., 22
Cullen, Dr. (Cardinal), 42, 55, 81
Delaney, Dr., 22, 23, 37, 41, 52, 55, 62, 71, 84
Dixon, Dr., 55
Egan, Dr., 22
Fitzgerald, Dr., 76
Foran, Dr., 22
Healy, Dr., 22
Hughes, Dr., O.S.F., 52
Kilduff, Dr., 55
Kinsella, Dr., 22
Kirby, Dr., 84
McCabe, Cardinal, 88
McCarthy, Florence, 52
Moriarty, Dr., 55
Moylan, Dr., 18, 19
Murphy, Dr., 22
Neville, Monsignor, 41
Newman, John H. (Cardinal), 48, 139

Other Bishops and Ecclesiastical Dignitaries, *contd.*—
Notary Apostolic, 9
O'Brien, Dean, Founder V.M.S., 54
Patrizi, Cardinal, 38, 39
Plunket, Oliver, 10
Prefect of Propaganda (Cardinal), 55
Sheehan, R. A., 71
Simeoni, Cardinal, 84
Walsh, Richard, 17
Ballymaloe, 121
Birmingham Oratory, 48
Bishops, five consecrated, 54
Blackletter-Bible, 125
Bloomfield, Dublin, 53
Bonsheim, 126
Bornheim, 14
Boureman, William, 6
Bradshaw, Sister Mary Letitia, 144
Bresnan, Thomas, 97, 98
Brooke, William, 65, 150
Burgundy, 136

C.

Canada, 81, 82
Cape of Good Hope, 46
Carlingford, 101
Cashel, 9, 29
Castlelyons, Dominican House of, vii., 127, 138
Catalogue of Convents in Ireland, 132
Chalice of Youghal, 124, 125, 126
Champsey, 43
Chapter General of Milan, 4
Rome, 5, 8, 10, 120, 128
Intermediate (Middle) of Ireland, 8, 68
Provincial of Dublin, 128
Provincial of Newbridge, 49
Chapter of Athenry, 12
Chancery, Master of, 150
Christian Brothers' Schools, 90
Chronicler of St. Mary's Cork, 61
CHURCHES—
St. Finbarr's West, 41
Franciscan, 13

Claddagh, 84
Cloyne, 2, 19, 55, 121
Coleraine, Dominican Community of, 5
Collins, Mrs., 120
Cologne, 4
Commissioners, Wide Street, 36
Committee of Butter Merchants, 49
Committee of House of Lords, 16
Congregation of Indulgences, Sacred, Rome, 22, 37
Constitutions of the Dominican Order, new edition, 51
Contents, ix.
Cork, Convent and Church of, xiii., 1, 2, 3, 4, 5, 12, 13, 17, 19, 21, 22, 24, 25, 26, 27, 29, 33, 34, 35, 36, 37, 39, 40, 42, 45, 46, 47, 48, 49, 55, 56, 59, 60, 63, 64, 65, 69, 70, 76, 86, 89, 97, 163
Coghlan, Rev. John (Ven. Archdeacon), 71, 102
Council General of Lyons, 3
Majesty's, 3
Privy, 10
Cromwell, 12
Cromwell's Cruelties, 128
Soldiers, 10
Usurpation, 11
Wars, 11
Crowe, Rev. John, P.P., 144
Custom House, Dublin, 38

D.

Daly & Son, Builders, 97
Daly, Rev Father, P.P., 41
Day, Robert, J.P., 126
Definition of the Immaculate Conception, 64
Demerara, 64
Dillon, Captain Arthur, 11
"Dominic of the Rosary," 94
Donegan, Daniel, J.P., 62
Drogheda, St. Catherine of Sienna, 54
Drogheda, St. Mary Magdalen, 64

Dromore, 53, 55, 66, 92, 96
Druineagh, 11
Dublin, Convent of St. Saviour's, 38, 48, 49, 66, 67, 80, 141
Pro-Cathedral, 55

E.

Ecclesiastics, Secular and Regular, whose names are attached to Address presented to Dr. Leahy, O.P., 58
Egan, John, 150
Elphin, 10
Emancipation Act, 19, 65, 90, 91, 140, 170 *et seq.*
Encumbered Estates Court, 49
Event of great importance, 5

F.

FEASTS:—
St. Athanasius of, 23
St. Luke of, 22
St. Patrick's Day, 47
Ferry, David, 4
Fitzgerald, John, 69
Franciscans, 130
French Revolution, 19
Friars Preachers, 600, and 43 Houses of, in Ireland, 10, 11
Friars Minors, 127, 128
Froude, James Anthony, 80

G.

Gaeta, 42
Galgey, John, 112
Galway, 12, 79, 80, 82, 136
Galwey, John G, 41
Garretstown, 10
Gibraltar, 52
Glanworth, Dominican House of, vii.
Convent of the Holy Cross, 131, 133, 138
Grammar School, Cork, 59
Guild of St. Thomas Aquinas—Young Men's Society 63

INDEX.

H.

Hall, Edwin, 2
Hanoverian Succession, 15
Hegarty, James and Patrick, 62
Hegarty, Patrick, 100
Hegarty, William, 2, 62
Hibernia Dominicana, xiv., 17, 46, 113, 120, 122, 130, 134, 181, 186, 192
Holy Cross Abbey, Tralee, 87, 88
Hospice of the Minerva, Rome, 49
House of Studies, 59, 61, 70
Hyland, O.S.F., Very Rev. Clement, 86

I.

Illustrations List of, xi.
Inscription, Latin, on inner Shrine of the Statute of our Lady of Youghal, 121

J.

Jandel's, Father, Letter to Community of St. Mary's, Cork, 60
Jesuits, The, and Monastic Orders, 20
Journal, Cork, Historical and Archæological, vii.
Ulster, of Archæology, 120

K.

Kanturk, 11
Keller, Canon (Ven. Archdeacon), P.P., 102
Kerry, 55, 94
Kinsale, 9, 13

L.

Languages, Hebrew and Greek, 50
Irish, 12
Leamlara, 47
Letter of the General of the Order, 60
Letter of Invitation to Synod of Thurles, 145

Limerick, Dominican Community of, 5, 63, 78, 79, 116
Lisbon, Irish College of Corpo Santo, 14, 18, 19, 40, 42, 48, 54, 71, 72, 90, 92, 94
Lismore, MS. of, 116
List of Deaths, 143
Louvain, Holy Cross Convent, 13, 18, 19, 47, 114
Low Countries, 14
Lurgan, 96
Lyons, Thomas, J.P., 62

M.

McCarthy, John G., 62
McCarthy, Michael, 16
McMullen, Barry, 69
Madras, 47
Madrid, Convent of the Most Blessed Virgin of Athoca, at, 135
Mahony, Timothy, J.P., 62
Mansion House, Cork, 56
Mathew Father, 56
Meeting, Important Public, 107
Memorable Document, 48
Memorial of the Regulars of Ireland addressed to Members of both Houses of Parliament, 146
Metz, 43
Missions, 55
Mitchelstown, 19
Murphy, John Count, D.L., 62, 97
Murphy, Nicholas, 97, 107, 112
Murphy, Nicholas Dan, 62
Murphy, Susan, 97
Murray, Maurice, D.L., 62

N.

Nagle, Councillor Joseph, 18
Nagle, Nano, 18
Nancy, Lorraine, 47
Newry, 84, 89, 95, 96
New Shrine, the Statute of Our Lady of Youghal, 123

INDEX.

NEWSPAPERS—
  Cork Examiner, 23, 74
  Cork Herald, 106
  Irish Catholic, 84
NOBILITY—
  Barry, David, 130
  Barry, John, 127
  Barry, Philip, Founder of "St. Marie's of the Isle," 1
  Barrymore, Lord, 128, 130
  Bourke, Sir William, 121, 122
  Boyle, Richard, the First Lord Cork, 116, 130
  Burgo, John de, 131
  Clanricarde, Earl of, 9
  Clare, Elizabeth de, 131
  Desmond, Countess of, 121, 122
  Desmond, Earl of, 116, 122
  Desmond, Sir James, 121, 122
  Desmond, Sir John, Dromana, 122
  Fitzgerald, Edmond, 121
  Fitzgerald, Honoria, daughter of James, 121, 122
  Fitzgerald, John, 121
  Fitzgerald, Maurice, 113
  Fitzgerald, Thomas, 113
  Geraldines, 114, 120
  Hore, Sir John, 122
  Inchiquin, Earl of, 8, 13
  James, the pretended Earl, 122
  King. Sir John, 7
  Lord President of Munster, 7
  Mortimer, Edmond, 4
  Roche, Raphael de la, 131
  Segar, Sir William, 131
  Vesey, William de, 114
Novitiate, Cork, 17, 61
  English Province, 80
  Irish, 80

O.

O'Brien, John, 16
Observance, Regular, 45, 61
Observance, Congregation of Strict, 5
O'Callaghan, Michael, 123
O'Connell, Daniel, The Liberator, 22
O'Connor, Denis, M.D., 62
O'Connor, Dr., O.S.A., 66
O'Sullivan, James, 100
O'Sullivan, Lawrence, 100

P.

Palencia, Old Castille, 136
Papal Commission, 51
Papal Rescripts, 37, 39
Parliament, Act of, 14
Peel, Sir Robert, 66
Penal Laws *versus* Dominican Fathers—Meeting at Chamber of Commerce, 167, 168
Perry Stephen, J.P., 112
Piazzia di Spagna, Rome, 63
Pistoris, Nicholas, 126
POPES —
  Clement IX., 15
  Gregory XVI., 22, 38
  Leo XIII., 76, 79, 100
  Paul III., 5
  Pius IV., 7
  Pius IX., 25, 27, 28, 42, 63, 74, 75
PRIESTS and Brethren of the Dominican Order—
  Ancarani, Father, 44
  Barrett, James, 15, 30
  Barry, Richard, 9, 29
  Barry, William, 13, 128
  Bonello, Father, 59
  Browne, John, 134
  Burke, Nicholas Thomas, 6, 61, 79, 80, 81, 86
  Butler, Lewis, 102
  Buttaoni, Father, 44
  Carbery James J, 42, 63, 69, 76, 77, 110, 121, 122
  Carroll, William Dominic, 64
  Condon, Cornelius Hyacinth, 60
  Conway, Antony, 143
  Conway, Father, 19
  Conway, Patrick Thomas, 64, 65, 68, 69, 71, 73, 150
  Costello, Father, 62
  Dean, Denis, 143
  Deely, James Thomas, 70

INDEX.

Priests and Brethren of the Dominican Order, *contd* --
Dunn, Patrick, 25
Dwyer, James A., 88, 100, 108
Fitzgerald, John, 17
Fitzgerald, Joseph Dominic, 64
Fitzgerald, Thomas, 11
Fleming, Walter, 14
Flood, P. V., 69
Flynn, James, 122
Frühwirth, Father, 96
Gibbon, Gerald, 134
Hanly, William, 143
Harold William V., 38, 53
Hennessy, Peter, 136
Hickey, Joseph Lewis, 70, 71, 141
Houghlahan, Dominic, 122
Howard, Father, 108
Hylan, Thomas, 17
Hyland, Thomas Raymond, 61, 69, 71
Jandel, Alexander Vincent, 42, 43, 44, 45, 46, 51, 60, 61, 64, 69, 70, 76, 80
Keane, M. A., 142
Kent, Richard, 12
Lacordaire, Père, 43, 44
Larocca, Joseph, 76, 96
Leahy, John Pius, 35, 38, 42, 49, 50, 53, 54, 55, 145
Littleton, James, 100
Loghlin, Thomas, 16
Lonergan, Patrick, 143
Lonergan, William, 18, 143
Lynch, John, 17, 18
McCarthy, Peter, 16
McCroghan, Eugene, 143
McCurtin, Dominic, 17
McDonnell, Daniel, 15
McGowan, Augustine Mathew, 100
Maguire, Eustace, 11, 29
Masterson, Father, 108
Mead, Michael, 143
Moore, James Michael, 101, 102, 141, 142
Moore, Matthias Gabriel, 101
Moral, Maurice, 4
Morrogh, Dominic, 17, 18, 143

Priests and Brethren of the Dominican Order, *contd*.--
Morrogh, John, 14, 29
Mullins, Patrick Thomas, 68
Mullooly, Joseph, 70, 84
Netterville, John Francis, 143
Nugent, Dr., 19, 47
Nugent, John, 143
O'Brian, John, 136
O'Brien, Daniel, 143
O'Brien, Daniel Albert, 17
O'Cahill, Æneas Ambrose, 10, 29
O'Callaghan Father, 69
O'Carroll, W. D., 64
O'Connell, P. J. Robert, 143
O'Connor, Ambrose, 15
O'Connor, John 35, 41, 62
O'Cuiffe, Constantius, 128
O'Daly, Dominic, 94
O'Fahadh, Raymond, 117
O'Garavain, Constantine, 134, 136
O'Garavain, Father, and his brother, 136, 137
O'Garavain, Peter, 14
O'Henny, James, 117
O'Heyn, John, 14, 117, 128, 134, 136, 137, 186
O'Kane, Father, 108
O'Keeffe, Constantine, 12
O'Kelly, Thomas, 122
O'Loughlin, Patrick Hyacinth, 143
O'Mahony, John, 18, 143
O'Morrogh, John, 8, 14, 29
O'Regan, John, 12
O'Ronain, Dominic, 117
Palmeggiani, Father, 44
Power, Bartholomew Hyacinth, 48, 62
Quinn, Father, 108
Roche, Aaron L., 35
Roche, David, 132
Roche, Theobald, 134
Roche, Richard, 47
Russell, Bartholomew Thomas, x, 2. 25, 35, 45, 46, 47, 48, 49, 55, 60, 65, 67, 69, 70, 90, 91, 92, 93, 99, 110, 121, 125, 150, 189

Priests and Brethren of the Dominican Order, *contd.*—
Ryan, John A., 35, 38, 52, 53, 54
San Vito, Joseph Maria, 70
Savage, John Lewis, 143
Scanlan, Richard Dominic, 68
Sheahan, John, 143
Sheehan, John, 19, 47
Towers, John Thomas, 88
Walshe, Lewis, 143
Walsh, Dominic, 17
Walsh, Father, 108
Walsh, Nicholas, 17
White, Robert Augustine, 45, 46, 48, 49, 63, 65, 150
Willard, John Thomas, 42, 62, 64, 89
Philadelphia, 54
Philippi, Nicolas, 126
Poor Clares, 95
Portico, St. Mary's, Cork, 63, 75
Presentation Monastery and Schools, 18
Priory, Pope's Quay, Cork, 2, 49, 56
Privy Council, 10
Propaganda, 54
Protest of Very Rev. B. T. Russell, 65
Provincial of England, 5
Provincial of Ireland, 12
Public Meeting in Chamber of Commerce, Cork, 68

Q.

Quercia La, "The Oak," Sanctuary of the Madonna, near Viterbo, 44
Quinlan, Jeremiah, 64, 150
Queenstown, 80

R.

Raleigh, Walter, 116
Raphoe, 55
Regicides, 29
Registry of Dominicans of Ireland, 13

Registry, Heraldic, of London, 131
Regulars, 11, 12, 20, 21, 68
Relief Bill, 20
Remhardi, Mark, 126
Revision of the Works of St. Thomas, 100
Roche, Alfred, Illustrations by, 115, 119, 129, 133, 135
Roche, James, 46, 120, 121
Rock of Cashel, 2, 9, 29
Rolls, Master of the — Important Charge, 64, 65, 150
Rolls, Patent, 116
Rome, 3, 42, 44, 60, 70, 77, 78, 83, 84, 88, 101
Rostrevor, 96
Rotterdam, 47
ROYAL PERSONAGES—
 Charles II., 11
 Edward I., 131
 Edward II., 3
 Edward III., 3
 Elizabeth, 7
 Henry VIII., 2, 5, 6, 116
 James I., 7
 James II., 13, 123, 128, 130
 Victoria, 23, 25
 William III., Prince of Orange, 7, 13
Royal Treasury, 3

S.

Sacred Palace, Rome, 44
San Luigi dei Francesi, Rome, 44
Santa Prassede, Rome, 40
See of Cashel, 2
 Cork, 17, 52
 Cloyne, 19
 Hamilton, Canada, 78, 79, 121
Seminaire Petit, Pont de Mousson, 43
Seminary, Ecclesiastical, 19
Seminary, Navan, 78
Sheyne, Matthew, Protestant Bishop, Cork, 7, 189
Simms, James Richard, 64, 150
Simms, Michael John, 65, 150

Sisters of Mercy, 95
Sligo, Dominican House, 114
Society of Jesus, 44
Society of St. Vincent de Paul, 97
Society, Young Men's, 54, 56, 63
Sodality of Holy Name, 98
Solemn Triduum, St. Mary's, Cork, 103
Spain, 15
Strasburgh, 126
St. Agnes, 38
St. Catherine, Dominican Church and Priory of, Newry, 96
St. Dominic, *title page*, 1, 51, 103
St. Francis of Assysium, 92
St. Ignatius, Exiled Sons of, 33
St. Mary's Collegiate Church, Youghal, 114
St. Mary's of the Isle, 2, 3, 5, 7, 11, 13, 26, 30, 47
St. Mary of Graces, Milan, 123
St. Paul, 51
St. Severus, 37, 38
St. Thomas, 50, 63, 71
St. Timothy, 51
Synod of Leinster, 55
Synod of Maynooth, 73
Synod, National, Thurles, 42, 94, 145

T.

Tallaght, St. Mary's, 61, 68, 81, 82, 83, 86, 141
Thickpenny, John, 116
Thurles, 42, 94
Toulouse, 13
Tralee, 55, 87, 114

Trinidad, 61, 64, 69, 88, 89
Twomey, Richard, 112

U.

United States, 64, 80

V.

Vicar-General, Circular Letter of, the Studies of the Order, 50
Victoria, Spain, 117
Viterbo, 44, 136

W.

Walsh, Rev. Maurice, P.P., 144
Walsh, William, 116
War of the Roses, 4
Westmeath, 78
Wide Street Commissioners, 36
Windele, John, son of the Cork Archæologist, 60
Woodchester, Gloucestershire, 80

Y.

YOUGHAL—
Chalice of, 124, 126
Dominican Convent of, 113
Dominican House of, vii., 101, 115, 117, 138
Franciscan Convent of, 101, 114
"Our Lady of Graces," 12, 102, 103, 113, 118, 122, 123, 125, 126, 186
Presentation Nunnery, 114

CORK: PRINTED BY GUY AND CO. LTD., 70, PATRICK STREET.

www.ingramcontent.com/pod-product-compliance
Lightning Source LLC
Chambersburg PA
CBHW020828230426
43666CB00007B/1144